SESSIONS WITH TIMOTHY AND TITUS

Smyth & Helwys Publishing, Inc.
6316 Peake Road
Macon, Georgia 31210-3960
1-800-747-3016
© 2006 by Smyth & Helwys Publishing
All rights reserved.
Printed in the United States of America.

The paper used in this publication meets the minimum
requirements of American National Standard for Information
Sciences—Permanence of Paper for Printed Library Materials.

Library of Congress Cataloging-in-Publication Data

McCullar, Michael, 1954–
Sessions with Timothy and Titus : timeless teachings for leaders of any age / Michael McCullar.
p. cm.
ISBN 1-57312-468-0 (pbk. : alk. paper)
1. Bible. N.T. Timothy—Textbooks. 2. Bible. N.T. Titus—Textbooks.
I. Title.

BS2745.55.M33 2006
227'.830071—dc22

2006029290

Sessions *with*
Timothy
&Titus

● ● ● Timeless *Teachings* for
Leaders of Any Age

Michael D. McCullar

SMYTH&HELWYS
PUBLISHING, INCORPORATED   MACON, GEORGIA

Acknowledgments

To Lisa, Mallory, and Jake for yet again enduring
a writing season . . . thanks for the support.

To Kris Peters for her support and assistance in the editorial
process and in the day-to-day structuring of my ministry.

To Mallory for her thoughtful critique of all things
grammar and syntax.

To Rickey Letson for taking time to read and
comment on this book.

To the people of Johns Creek Baptist Church for their
willingness to experience Sunday school in new
and creative ways.

To Smyth & Helwys for joining me in the vision for the
future of Sunday school through this series.

Table of Contents

Introducing 1 & 2 Timothy and Titus

Paul is the New Testament's most prolific writer and church evangelist. He wrote to inspire, teach, rebuke, and defend the gospel and his ministry. He wrote to churches and to individuals, and the totality of his work defined the role of apologist for Jesus Christ. Paul also provided much of the foundation for the formal study of theology. Over the years he has been equally lauded and condemned for his teachings on everything from the human sin condition to salvation by grace. The criticisms have been most intense on his views of women in the church and the lessened value of the Hebrew Law. A close study of Paul's teachings prove many of the criticisms to be hollow, even petty. However, that has not altered his polarizing impact on the church over time. Possibly Paul's greatest contributions have centered on the gospel being provided to the Gentiles and the creation of the church in the first century. Without Paul's intensity and myopic devotion to the progression of the gospel message, today's church might have developed differently.

Paul's letters to Timothy and to Titus are commonly referred to as the *Pastoral Epistles* and make up three of the four personal writings of Paul (the other being to Philemon). These letters are considered "pastoral" due to the nature of the writing and the specific roles being assigned to Timothy and Titus. Paul had mentored both men to varying degrees and had asked them to undertake difficult and challenging pastoral assignments. Timothy was given leadership of the internally troubled church in Ephesus that was suffering due to an influx of false teachers. Titus was sent to the island of Crete to reach the rough-and-tumble inhabitants known for their treachery and deceit. It is clear from Scripture that both men were young, lacked pastoral experience, and needed structured guidance and encouragement. Paul clearly addresses these needs in the pastoral letters, which demonstrates the value of teachings directed to individuals rather than the corporate church.

A consistent reality of Paul's ministry was his view of the imminent return of Christ and, thus, the end of this age. Above all others, this particular view frames his instructions both to pastoral leaders and to the church. Paul felt an urgency to equip the church for a ministry of reaching the Greco-Roman world for Christ. To this end, he wanted the church to be led by genuinely godly people who would ensure that all teaching was sound and uncompromised. This is clearly the case in the Pastoral Epistles, as his repetitive themes center on false teaching and the role of the church leader(s). In essence, these letters are primers on how to live lives of faith and how to deal with pernicious issues within the church. Despite the fact that the letters were written to specific groups in the first century, they hold universal value to modern church leaders as well.

Author and Date

Debates concerning the authorship of New Testament letters have raged for hundreds of years, specifically concerning Paul's contributions. Did Paul actually write all of the letters that bear his name? Could he possibly have written the volume of work attributed to him in the relatively short amount of time he served Christ? The easy and short answer to these authorship questions is yes, Paul actually wrote each letter bearing his name. This also seems to be the proper response to authorship questions of the Pastoral Epistles, as Paul cited himself as sender. It is also historically accurate that Paul had known Timothy and Titus for some time before assigning them to these specific ministry areas. Despite these known facts, scholars have nevertheless found much dissimilarity between the Pastoral Epistles and other works of Paul. Language patterns used in these letters are unique and would seem to be a shift in style for Paul. There also seems to be knowledge of events that might suggest a later date of authorship. Combined, however, these issues are rather easy to dispense with and do not lessen the likelihood of Paul being the author. The dates of the Timothy compositions seem to be approximately AD 64–65, with Titus written shortly thereafter. These dates would have been just prior to Paul's final imprisonment and death.

Recipients: Timothy and Titus

The Pastoral Epistles make up three of the four letters Paul wrote to individuals rather than churches. In each instance, Paul had known the person and had been pivotal in his profession of faith in Christ. In the case of Timothy, the relationship spanned many years and included his mother and grandmother. Timothy grew up in a household built on the devout Judaism of his mother Eunice and grandmother Lois. It appears his father was a Greek who professed neither Judaism nor Christianity, leading Timothy not to fully convert to Judaism as a child. During Paul's first visit to Lystra, Eunice and Lois converted to faith in Jesus Christ and became supporters of his ministry. Having been well-grounded in the Hebrew Scriptures by his family, Timothy was open to the message of Christ. He chose faith in Jesus during the first missionary visit by Paul, and by the second journey he had joined Paul as a church planter (Acts 16:1-3). Timothy's ministry experiences led him to assist churches in Philippi, Thessalonica, and Berea and later those in Corinth, Rome, and Ephesus. The Ephesus experience forms Paul's instructions in the Pastoral Epistles. Hebrews 13:23-24 cites Timothy's imprisonment (most likely in Rome), and tradition holds that Timothy was martyred during the time of emperors Domitian or Nerva (AD 90s).

Paul's second pastoral letter is directed to Titus, who had been assigned to the church on Crete. Oddly, Titus is not included in Acts in any form despite being given two major church responsibilities. Galatians 2:3 states Titus was a Greek Gentile who never converted to Judaism. Apparently he had come to faith in Jesus Christ under Paul's teaching and later joined him in missionary service. It is believed that he was a fervent disciple of Christ due to Paul's use of him as "a prime example of a Gentile convert worthy of acceptance by the church," as recorded in Galatians 2:1-5. The church in Jerusalem was still drawing distinctions between Hebrew converts and those coming from various Gentile backgrounds. Both Timothy and Titus were used to demonstrate the equality Paul found in the message of Christ. Titus's main contribution prior to Crete was to mediate the issues between Paul and the Corinthian church (2 Cor 7:6-16), which ironically was something Timothy was unable to accomplish. Titus was later chosen to return to Corinth to collect the delinquent missions offering for the Jerusalem church (2 Cor 8:6). At a point after his time in Crete he went to Rome to visit Paul and was sent to the church in Dalmatia. Tradition holds that Titus returned to Crete as an old man and was buried there.

Ephesus

During the time of Paul and Timothy, Ephesus was the Roman capital of Asia Minor and held the second largest population in the world. Ephesus carried the title "First and Greatest City of Asia Minor" and was home to dozens of shrines and temples to Greek and Roman gods. The largest pagan shrine in the world was built there to honor Diana, the goddess of the hunt and, later, goddess of motherhood. The Temple of Diana was listed as one of the original Seven Wonders of the World. It is reported that this temple would seat 25,000 people for events and ceremonies related to Diana worship. The temple was also home to varieties of sensual festivals involving male and female cult prostitutes that rivaled the ultra-sensual worship activities honoring Aphrodite in Corinth. Verses in Acts suggest that the Ephesian worship of Diana was seen as the greatest rival to the message of Christ in Rome (Acts 19:27-28). Later in the first century, people in Ephesus were mandated to worship emperors in temples dedicated to Vespasian and Domitian.

First-century Ephesus was a cultural and commercial center of great renown as it serviced Asia Minor east to west and allowed for sea travel on the Aegean. The city offered an advanced way of life in all areas with an exceptionally high standard of living. The city was also seen as one of the two greatest intellectual and political centers of the Aegean region. A large number of the successes of Ephesus can be traced back to the contributions of Alexander the Great, who spent time and resources on the city.

Crete

Crete is the fifth largest island in the Mediterranean and the largest of the Greek Isles. The island is uniquely narrow and straight, stretching 150 miles in length from east to west and varying in width from 7.5 to 35 miles. Crete is also framed by four severe mountain ranges that spring up from the sea, the highest point reaching 8,000 feet. Crete is actually more famous for the activity of Greek gods and deities than for natural occurrences. It is boasted that Zeus resided on Crete with his bride Europa and is buried on the island. The Minoan period is a celebrated era for Cretans, but is one based more on the exploits of King Minos, son of Zeus and

Europa, than on classical Greek progress. Inhabitants of Crete were also well known for lying, cheating, boisterous behavior, and drinking alcohol, leading to the derogatory phrase "behaving like a Cretan." Amazingly, the church on Crete became one of the most successful first- and second-century fellowships.

Occasion of the Letters

First Timothy was written to train and encourage Timothy in his assignment as the new leader of the Ephesian church. Timothy was challenged to rid the church of false teachers and the subsequent immorality, to heal divisions, to strengthen and sustain the role of women in the church, to provide a structure for church functions, and to create a template for dealing with the various age groups in the church. Second Timothy was a second letter to Timothy coming near the end of Paul's life. Paul's tone is reminiscent and almost sad in portions of the writing, but in total it is a continuation of the initial letter of encouragement and instruction.

Titus was written to its namesake, who took over the leadership of the church on Crete. It is thought to have been written simultaneously with the first Timothy letter. Titus was charged with many of the same responsibilities as Timothy, even though the church landscapes were quite dissimilar. One difference is found in Titus's charge to expand the church on the island, effectively planting multiple fellowships throughout Crete. Many other themes are repetitions of those found in both Timothy letters, making the Pastoral Epistles almost interchangeable throughout.

Sessions with Timothy and Titus

The False Teachers of Ephesus

Session 1

1 Timothy 1:3-10; 6:3-5

In today's church, the arrival of a new minister is often a time of celebration and hope for the future. The newly installed spiritual leader is honored and enjoys the luxuries of a "honeymoon" period. Some churches even continue to provide what is known affectionately as an "old-fashioned pounding" for the new ministry family. This practice dates well back and has a long history of providing for the basic start-up needs of the new minister. Unfortunately, this practice does not stretch back as far as Timothy's time serving the church in Ephesus. The "pounding" he received in Ephesus was most certainly not of the loving and equipping kind.

The Ephesus church was going through a difficult period and was virtually teeming with theological and relational problems and issues. Internal and external problems and issues literally tore at the foundations of the Ephesian fellowship. The problems common to these Christians focused on false teaching and bad theological practices, infusions of ancient practices, church order, and the roles of men and women in the church. During this divisive period, Paul assigned Timothy to lead the dysfunctional and struggling church, granting him authority and command over the entire fellowship of new believers. Paul obviously knew that it was imperative for someone to take charge and rid the church of sinister (even if only misguided) elements and provide proper theological structure.

Timothy's first and foremost challenge was to deal with the rash of false teachings that were negatively impacting the church fellowship. False teaching was neither new nor unique to Ephesus. Jesus warned of false teachers, as did most of the other New Testament teachers and writers. Paul dealt strongly with such issues in both the Galatian and Corinthian letters, coining a term denoting the contrary nature of the false theology. This "different gospel" was a desertion of the overall gospel of Christ and also promoted a "different Jesus" and a "different spirit" (2 Cor 11:1). Paul uses a Greek verb in 1 Timothy 1:3 to show that these teachers had indeed deviated form the norm of New Testament teaching. Multiple times in the letters to Timothy and Titus, Paul cites "the faith," "the truth," "sound doctrine," "the teaching," and "the good deposit," contrasting Paul's view of the gospel message with the newly minted versions.

Paul clearly drew the battle lines and provided Timothy with almost unprecedented pastoral authority to deal with the crippling problems of the Ephesus church. In the process of assigning blame and selecting Timothy, he neglected to offer specifics as to the identity and actual message of the deviant teachers. Itinerant teachers and philosophers were common during that era in Greco-Roman cities, and most offered unique perspectives, questions, and views. In reality, it was most likely unnecessary to be overly specific with either Timothy or other sympathetic church leaders. They knew the problem people and the degrees of false theology being proffered. Plus, Paul had a tendency to focus on the particular church to which he was writing and did not seem to have a genuine future view of the church. Paul labored under the assumption of the imminent return of Christ and thus would not have envisioned the church of one hundred years hence, and certainly not the passage of two millennia.

False Doctrine

The base charge of teaching false doctrine seems a convenient "one-size-fits-all" indictment against those Timothy was charged with silencing. It is true that Paul was not specific in spelling out the heresy, but that fact in no way lessens the problem. Paul used strong language to emphasize the strength of Timothy's charge to silence those teaching contrary truths. To designate Timothy's new role, Paul used the Greek verb "command" multiple times. This is the same word Jesus used in sending forth the disciples and in defending his own ultimate authority. With this verb used to assign Timothy, it is unlikely that anyone missed the serious nature of his calling and position.

The phrase "teaching false doctrines" is used again in 1 Timothy 6:3 and represents Paul's use of repetition to emphasize the full impact of issues. It would be easy, however, to miss the depth of this particular phrase due to translational shortcomings. The original language implies something much greater than "different" in regards to teaching, with "totally and completely false" being more accurate. In combining 1 Timothy 1:3 with 6:3, a more accurate rendering would be "to teach in contrast to the sound instruction of our Lord Jesus Christ to Godly teaching" (Liefield, 53).

This would strongly suggest that the instruction was not only different but also completely false. This reality is backed up by Paul's similar statements in Galatians 1:6-8, where he writes that a "different gospel" is really " no gospel at all" and that those who espouse it should be "eternally condemned." Paul's strong language highlights the growing problems within the Ephesus church but does little to confine the heresies to a specific, competing group. It is possible that these teachings were so complex that they were the result of multiple offenders and not simply one philosophy or quasi-theology. To that end, the following are possibilities of unorthodox and heretical elements known to have infested the early church; those prone "to myths, fables and endless genealogies, those who promote controversies, and those who want to be teachers of the law but who know nothing" (1 Tim 1:4-7).

GNOSTICISM

The distinctly Greek system of belief known as Gnosticism was the single worst internal enemy of the church through the second century. While there were several groups and lines of thought that represented one of the above indictments, Gnosticism included virtually all of them. The basic belief of Gnosticism was that all matter is essentially evil and only the spirit is good. Since matter was both preexistent and inherently evil, tainted matter was used to create the world. The natural consequence of this belief is that God could not have been a direct part of the creation process since God cannot abide evil. In order to pull off this feat, God would have been forced to separate from the process by sending out a series of emanations, or lower gods, to do the heavy lifting. Each emanation would distance itself from the original until one emanation would be so distant from God that it could effectively create the world. Since these emanations were forced to spawn additional emanations in order to create from flawed matter, the spiritual world would literally be filled with huge numbers of lesser gods. Gnostics also believed that as each emanation descended further from God, it became less and less like God, eventually resulting in a series of gods who were more evil than holy.

The reality of hostile lower gods also factored into the ways humans could be saved. Gnostics saw God as not only distant from creation but also wholly disinterested in its result. This negative reality factored heavily into the path to salvation for humankind. In order for individuals to achieve salvation, they would be forced to maneuver the labyrinth of emanations in order to reach the ultimate, yet uninvolved God. In essence, everyone would be left to his or her own devices as God would not reach out and assist in the salvation process. This tenet of Gnostic theology resulted in a form of intellectual elitism that favored the initiated over the functionally ignorant and uninformed. A true Gnostic was privy to a unique, special knowledge (gnosis) that was required to reach God. The need for this secretive and privately held knowledge was the main teaching point of the Gnostics as they invaded the early church.

As for Paul's complaint of being concerned with "fables and endless genealogies" (1 Tim 1:4), Gnostics provided each emanation a lineage and personal history. This practice sought to legitimize the multiplicity of gods in an otherwise monotheistic faith. Gnostics also taught that the spirit alone was good and instructed married people to abstain from marital relations in order to protect their spiritual lives. This was followed by strict dietary codes forbidding the consumption of meat, again due to the evil of the flesh and the need to remove one's self from unnecessary evils. The entire doctrine of Gnosticism became fixated on the dangers of giving in to the tainted, flawed, and inherently sinful human element. Rather than lead people to find the beauty in creation, Gnostics sought to suppress actions and activities that Jesus, Paul, and other New Testament voices proclaimed as God's purpose and plan for humankind. Obviously, these myriad teachings led to long bouts of arguments and controversies, which was another indictment Paul leveled against the false teachers in Ephesus.

GREEK INTELLECTUALS

Three hundred years before Christ, Greece was positioned as the seat of knowledge and learning. From its inception with Plato and Socrates, Greek intellectualism spread into the wider world as the primary style of discourse. The use of logic became the template for debate over life's meaning, and it quickly spread into religious circles. Being purely rational in nature, Greek intellectualism denied the possibility of a resurrection of the physical body. Since dead people did not routinely rise from the tomb and resume life where they left off, it is easy to see how the linear-thinking Greeks would have discounted the story of Jesus. The enormous leap of faith required for a rationally trained intellectual to believe that Jesus died a human but arose a god led to few early converts among the intelligentsia.

There were over time, however, many Greeks who did convert and make the shift to the miraculous nature of Christ. Imagine the difficulties of a Greek convert who accepted Christ in all his forms, only to be later taught within the church that the resurrection was not an actual event. This was one type of pernicious teaching that grew more and more intense within the early church due to humanistic reasoning. Paul pointed out this dilemma in the first Corinthian letter:

> Where is the wise man? Where is the scholar? Where is the philosopher of this age? Has God not made foolish the wisdom of the world? Jews demand miraculous signs and Greeks look for wisdom, but we preach Christ crucified; a stumbling block to Jews and foolishness to Gentiles, but to those whom God has called, both Jews and Greeks, Christ the power of God and the wisdom of God. For the foolishness of God is wiser than man's wisdom, and the weakness of God is stronger than man's strength. (1 Cor 1:20, 22-25)

The issue of intellect over base-level supernatural faith was both real and intense during Paul's time with the Ephesian church. Much like Gnosticism, this issue took real prisoners and left great damage in its wake. Paul even took the unusual step of throwing Hymenaeus and Alexander out of the church for teaching contrary to the resurrection of Christ (1 Tim 1:19). Paul told the Corinthians that the resurrection is the epicenter of Christianity and thus non-negotiable for the gospel to have integrity. Without the resurrection, however humanly illogical and irrational it remains, faith in Christ is compromised beyond repair.

GENEALOGISTS AND WANNABE TEACHERS

There was a fascination in the Ephesian church with genealogies that Paul deemed "endless" (1 Tim 4:1; 4:7; Titus 3:9). Gnostics utilized elaborate historical family lines to support their belief in multiple lower gods (emanations), but other factions within the early church also promoted genealogical importance. Hebrews placed great value on genealogies and took pride in aligning themselves with the patriarchs and tribes. To the classic Hebrew mind, one's pedigree was based as much on lineage as on character, which explains the abundance of "begets" in the Old Testament. Matthew uses genealogy to justify Jesus as coming from the line of David. By the first century, Hebrews were guilty of overemphasizing genealogical purity and, in essence, of rewriting history. The Book of Jubilees and the Biblical Antiquities both revise Hebrew history through genealogy in order to preserve the original calling of Israel and status of the Mosaic Law (Stott, 44). Another example of genealogical abuse is the extensive history provided Enoch, despite his being featured prominently in but one verse.

Paul cites additional problems stemming from "those who want to be teachers of the law but who do not know what they are talking about" (1 Tim 1:7). It appears a faction of would-be teachers were holding on to the trappings of the original Hebrew Law and infusing its necessary adherence into the Christian faith equation. Identical problems with Judaizers, those who sought to force Hebrew practices onto Gentile converts to Christ, were prevalent in every church setting of the day. Judaizers espoused requiring Gentiles to become Jews before being baptized, even to the point of ritual circumcision. Paul's stock answer for them was simply to cease and desist as the Law of Moses no longer applied to the new believer. When Jesus stated, "I have not come to destroy the law but to fulfill it" (Matt 5:17), he effectively closed the door on the need for the Old Testament law. In his reasoning, Paul did not jettison the law; rather, he simply shifted the purpose of the law to the "unrighteous" (1 Tim 1:9). The law could now provide purpose to the sinner and the godless by offering structure for proper comportment and the possibility of finding God.

Timothy Versus the False Teachers

There is no getting around the fact that Timothy was quite young and inexperienced and, in many ways, questionable for such a challenge as the Ephesus church. Despite having grown up with Lois and Eunice and having a thorough knowledge of the Hebrew Scripture, nothing Timothy had done earlier in life had prepared him for this role. Therefore, Paul encouraged him to "fight the good fight, holding on to faith and a good conscience" (1 Tim 1:18-19).

In essence, Paul declared that Timothy's greatest strengths for his upcoming theological battles were his strong faith and moral purity. Many in the new fellowship had already strayed and compromised their spiritual vitality due to the false teachers. They had become easy marks for the evil found in the erroneous teaching and had grown disruptive within the church. Timothy was to combat this with sound teaching, love, and patience. Bad theology may enter with haste but will never leave with like speed. Maximus of Tyre said, "God is the general; life is the campaign; man is the soldier" (Barclay, 58). Timothy would be committing for the long haul and would need to be the strongest force within the church. Paul provided sound encouragement and instruction for Timothy, which, combined with the wisdom of the Holy Spirit and excellence in modeling the faith, would provide Timothy with all he needed to make a profound difference in Ephesus.

Life Lessons

Paul assigned Timothy and Titus to the difficult tasks of leading troubled churches that were rife with false teaching and general immorality. Of course, this was nothing new in Greek culture as most religions were sensually and intellectually based, but Paul was never one to settle for the ordinary. He had already established that the church built on Jesus Christ was to be different in virtually every way from the religious order of the day, specifically in theology and lifestyle. It was Timothy's job to eradicate the morally deficient teachers from the church and to teach proper theology to the new believers. His success would allow for the church to grow and mature spiritually in preparation for reaching the Greco-Roman world for Christ.

History demonstrates that the early church did indeed mature and become a world-shaping force for Christ. The early believers successfully navigated barriers and enemies by immersing themselves in proper doctrine, theology, and spiritual practices. Rather than relying on intellect and reason, which was the accepted norm, they opted for trust, faith, and love. They countered their hostile society by demonstrating faith based on love. This was a truly unique way to live life. Sadly, it still is.

The modern church should adopt the Ephesian template for impacting the world with an inclusive and equitable message. It is time to be intentional about this due to the gross negativity present in today's Christian message. Today's church will never be effective in impacting religious pluralism if battle lines are drawn at the expense of dialogue. Add to this the high number of splits and schisms and the worldwide church landscape is an absolute mess. The best answer continues to be Paul's instruction to Timothy to teach the truth with love. Love-based ministry worked in Ephesus and on Crete, and it will work today if we will avail ourselves to its simple power.

1. Describe problems Timothy faced in the Ephesus church.

_____

_____

_____

_____

_____

_____

2. How would you describe and define a cult belief?

_____

_____

_____

_____

_____

_____

3. In what ways did myths and endless genealogies lead to false teaching?

_____

_____

_____

_____

_____

_____

4. Describe the differences between Greek philosophy and Christian theology.

_____

_____

_____

_____

_____

_____

5. List the tenets of Gnosticism.

_____

_____

_____

_____

_____

_____

6. In what ways did Greek intellectualism differ from Paul's teaching on Christ?

_____

_____

_____

_____

_____

_____

7. Who were the Judaizers and what did they teach?

_____

_____

_____

_____

_____

_____

8. Describe why love is the best weapon against bad theology.

_____

_____

_____

_____

_____

_____

To Pray Like Paul

In the initial chapter of the Timothy letters, Paul dispenses with the issues related to the law and purely false doctrines. He establishes that the scope and range of the church's responsibility is far greater than the limited and finite rationale of the Gnostics. The same short-sided thinking could be applied to the Judaizers who saw the path to salvation requiring a stopover in the Mosiac Law. Paul widened the path to salvation to include everyone and claimed that the church is responsible for progressing this inclusionary plan of God. Initially the Hebrews were created to be a "Holy Nation and a Nation of Priests" (Exod 19:6), effectively becoming the chosen route for God's reconciliation of the world. Over time, Israel became selfish and exclusive, effectively deeming most other people groups as unworthy of God's equal love and salvation. This shift to *being god* rather than *obeying God* led to the spiritual paralysis of Israel. God's plan then shifted to the Messiah Jesus and the final sacrifice that provided salvation to all people. Galatians 3:28 functions as the Magna Carta of the faith: "There is neither Jew nor Greek, there is neither slave nor free, there is neither male nor female; for you are all one in Christ Jesus." Paul's use of the Greek noun *everyone* "can be better rendered *all kinds of people*, and *all* often refers inclusively to classes of people" (Baugh, 453). Lost in the "Chosen People" focus on Israel is the fact that God meant from the very first moment to include Gentiles: "And the scripture, foreseeing that God would justify the Gentiles by faith, preached the gospel to Abraham beforehand, saying, 'in you all nations shall be blessed'" (Gal 3:8).

A casualty of the increasingly myopic stance of the Hebrews was the practice of prayer in the lives of individual believers. The entirety of the faith practices of the Jews had, over time, become overly corporate. Atonement and providence were celebrated more in the corporate observance than in the individual heart, leading to prayer practice becoming much more rote than alive and fresh. Blame it on the "hardened hearts" of Israel or on the voluminous law then in place, but either way prayer had suffered in the process. This is why the model prayer of Jesus (Matt 6:9-13) was so progressive in its focus on the individual believer. Faith practice was now individual-to-God in intent, scope, and function. Paul rarely commanded anything of his readers that he had not already established as his own life's practice. He seemed to exist on the strength found in his communion with God. Even a cursory reading of Paul's work will provide a model of piety and power rooted in prayer, especially the selfless approach he writes of in each letter. Add in the dangerous calling he boldly endured as chief evangelist to a hostile world and one sees how prayer powers vision, calling, and commitment. Paul commanded this type of prayer practice of the Ephesian believers.

How to Pray

Paul begins the second chapter with a unique diagram of prayer as four components: *requests, prayers, intercession,* and *thanksgiving.* By utilizing this fourfold definition, he breaks with any notion of prayer being simply unilateral conversation with God. Paul is describing an act of being involved with God. Kenneth Leech, British spiritual director, defines prayer as participating in God:

> The God of Christian prayer is an involved God, a social God. Involvement and society are among the essential marks of Christian prayer because prayer is actually a participation in God. God is involved in humanity, and so prayer is an involvement in humanity. God is social and not isolated, and so prayer is a social, not an isolated, activity. (8)

Leech goes on to state that "prayer is the movement of God to humankind and of humankind to God, the rhythm of encounter and response" (8). This intimate communion with God through prayer is the foundational practice of effective faith development. Sadly, if a modern believer was asked which faith practice was most important, he or she would likely respond "evangelism." While it is hard to vote against evangelism, in this case it would be the wrong answer. To Paul, prayer is the first priority, and all other faith expressions sequence and flow from the encounter with God.

> The church is essentially a worshipping, praying community. It is often said that the church's priority task is evangelism. But this is really not so. Worship takes precedence over evangelism, partly because, long after the church's evangelistic task has been completed, God's people will continue to worship him eternally, and partly because evangelism is itself an aspect of worship. (Stott, 59)

REQUESTS

Paul begins his practical lesson on personal prayer by first citing *requests* made to God. This seems to be a selfish start to a time of intimate communion with God. What about worship? Doesn't the Model Prayer begin with a focus on God? Doesn't the age-old A. C. T. S. formula (*acknowledgment, confession, thanksgiving, supplication*) begin with acknowledging God and end with requests? Yes, there is no getting around the fact that Paul's landmark teaching on prayer does indeed begin with one asking rather than praising God.

Paul, however, seems to be orthodox in this teaching by seeing prayer as an act of worship. It is possible that one facet of pure theology found here is that personal worship and personal prayer are synonymous. By going back to Leech's classic approach of prayer being "the rhythm of encounter and response" (8), it becomes easier to see the totality of the prayer experience as being worship. If this were a true interpretation, then it would be all but impossible to err in beginning the prayer experience with requesting things from God. This elevates the communication from selfish to purely personal.

Requests or supplications, then, are merely asking God to meet certain, specific needs. Early theologian Origen defines supplication as "making earnest requests amid personal need" (14). John Wesley, founder of Methodism, adds, "Supplication is the imploring of help in time of need" (774). This component has the effect of demonstrating how utterly dependent individual believers are on God. Scottish theologian William Barclay notes, "Prayer must begin with a sense of need and must include our own personal sense of inadequacy" (65). Requests are the component of prayer that not only demonstrates our place before God, but also God's providential power. It is as if each person's weaknesses and needs become God's power in and through the prayer act.

PRAYERS

The second component of prayer listed by Paul is labeled *prayers*. The basic difference between the Greek words translated *requests* and *prayers* is that the former can be used to address both people and God, while the latter is used only as an approach to God. William Barclay writes, "There are certain needs, which can only be brought to Him. There is strength, which He alone can give; a forgiveness, which He alone can grant; a certainty, which He alone can bestow" (66).

There is unusually wide agreement among scholars that this component of prayer is the most intensely intimate of the four. This element instills a sense of awe and reverence as God is approached and worshiped. In a uniquely spiritual way, it is a reversal of Hosea 11:9 where God states, "I am God and not man: the Holy One in the midst of you." It is in *prayer* that we indicate to God, "I am human and not God. I am unholy, yet I am saved by grace as I stand in the midst of the Holy One." Quite possibly, it is in this element of the prayer act that we are most spiritually attuned to God's presence and providence. It is easy to imagine Moses kneeling before the manifestation of God in the burning bush and being in *prayer*. Also, after Isaiah encounters God in *prayer*, he accepts his calling by responding, "Here am I. Send me!" (Isa 6:8).

INTERCESSION

Paul's third component of prayer is *intercession*. The Greek noun used for intercession is found only twice in the New Testament, with both instances being in the Timothy letters. This scarcity of usage does not diminish the word or lessen the importance of the practice; rather, it suggests that the full scope of prayer was rarely dealt with in Scripture. However, the practice of intercession in general is not foreign to Scripture, nor is it difficult to explain. Walter Liefeld defines intercession succinctly as "offering petitions on behalf of others" (85). G. W. Knight adds, "Appealing boldly on behalf of others" (115). Ancient writer Theodore of Mopsuestia elevates the idea as "seeking freedom from undeserved consequences" (Gorday, 153).

The main difference between intercession and the other components is in the direction of focus and intent. Rather than focus intently on either our own needs or on the majesty of God, intercessory prayer is all about the needs of other people. Jesus acts as an intercessor for humankind on a constant basis: "Who will bring a charge against God's elect? It is God who justifies. Who is he who condemns? It is Christ who died, and furthermore is also risen, who is even at the right hand of God, who also makes intercession for us" (Rom 8:33-34). The key to effective intercession is to attend fervently to the needs of others through prayer, on their behalf, and not to allow our personal issues to monopolize the prayer process. Intercession, thus, becomes an act of *agape*-love, where the needs of others are promoted over those of the person praying. "Intercessions are prayers offered, not for us, but for others, in which the suppliants, looking out from themselves upon the needs of all classes and conditions of men, make petitions for others in special need" (Harvey, 29).

Kenneth Leech deals with a longstanding question concerning intercession: "If God knows what is going to happen, what is the point of asking?" (24). He goes on to say that intercession is an act of "co-operation" between a person and God on behalf of others (24).

> The fact that God knows whether we should be wet or dry does not prevent us from taking an umbrella. Clearly God is allowing us to influence the course of events. For we are not robots, and the world is not a machine. Intercessory prayer is not a technique for changing God's mind, but it is a releasing of God's power through placing ourselves in a relationship of co-operation with God. It is an act. It *is* action. Intercession means literally to stand between, to become involved in the conflict. (Leech, 24-25)

THANKSGIVING

The final component of prayer is *thanksgiving*. With this element, we conclude the encounter with God, effectively shifting away from needs (ours and others') to the blessings provided us by God. William Barclay states, "Prayer does not only mean asking God for things; prayer also means thanking God for things" (67). Effective thanksgiving requires a working knowledge of blessings received over time. This is possibly why so many people complain of bogging down when focusing on past blessings in prayer and opt for the catchall "Thank you for all my bountiful blessings!"

Paul would disagree with the "shortcut" approach and opt for the prominence of listing all blessings during the prayer act. Is it possible to remember *all* of our blessings, much less recite them during prayer? Realistically, no. It is unlikely that anyone would have that much command over the memory process or the time to spend in prayer. These realities do not mean, however, that we shouldn't try to meet the lofty standards of full prayer. The fact that the bar has been placed incredibly high simply signals the importance of the goal. R. C. Tench notes, "Regarded as one manner of prayer, it (thanksgiving) expresses that which ought never be absent from any of our devotions, namely the grateful acknowledgment of past mercies as distinguished from the earnest seeking of future ones" (191).

Jane E. Vennard writes and teaches on prayer. In her book, *A Praying Congregation*, she writes that expressing gratitude should be an integral part of our humanness and, thus, our prayer lives. If this is difficult to include in either life or prayer, she suggests keeping a prayer journal that focuses on blessings and gratitude. By doing this she believes a person can grow in capacity to see and record joy (129). Obviously thanksgiving must be intentional and well practiced. When true thanksgiving is accomplished, it can elevate the entirety of a person's spiritual life.

For Whom to Pray

Paul shifts from defining prayer as four components to stipulating specifics on for whom to pray. He clearly moves beyond the fallacy that *everyone* actually includes everyone when it comes to prayer. In 2:1-2, he commands prayer for *all* people, specifically kings and all who are in authority. The ramifications of this instruction are huge. In the act of intercession, all people must be lifted up to God as a part of the prayer act. Inherent in Christian intercession is the idea that the people prayed for are actually loved or, at least to some degree, appreciated. By including kings and all people in authority, Paul added an additional degree of difficulty to an already unnatural act. To move beyond the personal needs of the praying person is an act of selflessness, but to do so for a ruthless, pagan emperor was beyond comprehension. *Pray for Nero?! You must be kidding me!*

Paul did indeed have Nero and other Roman, Greek, and Hebrew rulers in mind with this command. At this time in history, there were no Christian rulers in existence in any place in the known world. The early believers were under growing persecution from Rome and the hostile Jews, both of whom would turn on the church with unprecedented ferocity just six to eight years later. Much of the false teaching plaguing the Ephesus church came from Greek religions, and these people would have also been included in

Paul's admonition for intercession. What did Paul have in mind as he penned these words? Intercession for the demise of the hostile leaders? Plagues of boils and locust?

No; Paul did have classic intercession in mind, but the motives were the slightest bit slanted toward the church. His rationale is voiced in verse 2: ". . . that we may lead a quiet and peaceable life in all godliness and reverence." In verse 4 he expands the goal to include all people coming to a saving knowledge of Jesus Christ. It is not only about good governance resulting in a spiritual *Pax Romano* (Peace of Rome); it is about an orderly society in which the church can effectively be the presence of Christ. If government worked at its effective best, so could the church. It is true that Paul held no genuine future view for the church due to his belief in the imminent return of Christ. He did, however, have an excellent short-term vision for all the church could accomplish if there was no interference from hostile rulers.

It cannot be overstated that the emperor of Rome at this time was the infamous Nero. It would be difficult to find a ruler more ruthless than Nero. He was reported to be pathologically unsound, thought himself to be a god, and was a serial murderer. He even killed his own family due to his egomaniacal paranoia. He executed Christians to cover up for his complicity in the burning of much of Rome, impaling them on stake-like poles and setting them on fire. It is commonly held that Nero executed Paul despite the privilege and protections of Paul's Roman citizenship. All of this would have been common knowledge among believers, making this form of prayer one of the toughest, most sacrificial requirements in all of Scripture. Yet, Paul was unflinching in his command to pray for and honor all positions of societal and governmental leadership. The faith goal promoted by Paul disallowed the natural negative hatred and resentment felt toward those who exemplify gross evil. God's expressed goal is for all people to come to faith and salvation through Christ. This includes people like Nero. God's grace is that wide and encompassing. Plus, if the society in which the church exists is stable, the church can get on with the business of doing what the church does best—being salt and light to a genuinely dark and needy world.

Life Lessons

Prayer is to the spiritual life as oxygen is to the physical life: absolutely necessary. It would seem impossible for a person to grow in spiritual maturity, or to find God's will for life, outside of active prayer. Jesus provided the Model Prayer in his teaching in order to promote the personal relationship over the more corporate Hebrew practice, but he never intended for his words to be adopted in rote form for rote recitation. Where in such a memorization process is the personal encounter that should be freshly new and energized with each encounter? Perhaps Kenneth Leech's view of prayer as "the movement of God to humankind and of humankind to God, the rhythm of encounter and response" (8), best speaks to the interconnectedness of the prayer act. It certainly seems that the largest barrier to effective prayer practice could be the unilateral approach many people adopt. When prayer becomes a personal mantra or something that can be recited during sleep, possibly the entire practice has been corrupted beyond the biblical mandates. Leech is simply using the teachings of Paul, who adapted the teachings of Jesus, to state that prayer is to be undertaken by the individual in order to engage the involvement of God. As God engages, the reality of each aspect of encounter will initiate response. Simply put, prayer that is biblically genuine is not to be a monologue or a recitation of fancy prose aimed at sounding spiritual to a faraway God. It is to be a frank, intimate, and personal approach to God, who responds when engaged.

It is also important to state that while structure can be abused, format and structure are important. People seem to have few problems beginning a prayer. But what follows "Dear God, forgive me and provide for me" is up for grabs. This is why the now ancient A.C.T.S. model of prayer has been popular for such a long time. It provides for basic flow and structure.

In this section, however, we have Paul's in-depth structuring of the prayer act that can be easily adapted by those seeking assistance with structure and content. The beauty in Paul's method for prayer is that a person can find structure plus a spiritual path of entreaty with God. Paul seems to recognize that rote prayers are the result of content issues, not structure. By praying in requests (general needs), prayers (specific needs), intercession (for others), and thanksgiving (recognizing God's contributions), the person moves toward an advancing God. Effective, life-changing communion begins as God and the individual come together. So the secret to great prayer is not in the language or structure; it is found in a combination of format and content. Of course, attitude and earnestness also factor in, as each person must both sense and act upon the need to seek God.

Prayer in any format must be God-centered and must never fall prey to the selfish want or need possible in everyone.

1. In your view, what is the single biggest barrier to effective personal prayer? Explain.

_____
_____
_____
_____
_____
_____

2. Interpret each of Paul's prayer components in one sentence as if explaining them to another person.

_____
_____
_____
_____
_____
_____

3. Explain ways in which a person could begin prayer with requests but also worship and praise.

_____
_____
_____
_____
_____

4. Cite possible difficulties in praying for "those in authority," specifically those who abuse freedom and rights.

_____
_____
_____
_____
_____

5. What do you see as Paul's motivations behind the command to pray for kings and leaders of the Greco-Roman world?

_____
_____
_____
_____
_____
_____

6. Explain prayer using Kenneth Leech's definition of "the movement of God to humankind and of humankind to God, the rhythm of encounter and response" (8).

_____
_____
_____
_____
_____
_____

7. Which is easiest, praying for one's own needs or interceding on behalf of others? Explain.

_____
_____
_____
_____
_____
_____

8. List ways for improving the thanksgiving component in prayer.

_____
_____
_____
_____
_____
_____

Men and Women in the Church

Paul continues his instruction to Timothy and the Ephesian church with a shift to the manner and function of prayer. Earlier he spent time breaking an effective, genuine prayer into components, focusing primarily on content. Here we see Paul move into the public arena, first on prayer in public by men, and then into an unusually long teaching on the behavior and fitfulness of women in worship settings. H. H. Harvey denotes this section heading as "Position and Duties of the Sexes in the Worship of the Public Assembly" (32). I would opt for a much less formal and heady title such as "One Thing Men Must Do and Many Things Women Must Not Do in Public Worship in Ephesus"!

As is the case with most of Paul's writings concerning women, this section has generally been taken to mean that women have fewer rights and subsequent opportunities within the church. Due to the tendency of people throughout history to take his work with literal seriousness, Paul is simultaneously lauded and vilified for his words here and elsewhere concerning women. This is especially true of this chapter with its restrictions on praying, teaching, and even speaking in the worship setting, not to mention the difficult-to-decipher teaching on Eve and childbirth. Thomas Oden cites the health hazards related to Paul's words concerning women in these verses: "This paragraph of Paul's letter to Timothy cannot be read without raising hackles and blood pressure" (93). Suffice it to say that hypertension is but one of the negatives flowing from Paul's take on women in the Ephesus church.

Entire doctrinal philosophies and structures have been created, implemented, and supervised due to this chapter, resulting in women in many faith walks being restricted from official service positions. Ordination for women has also been greatly affected by the writings of Paul, especially the Timothy letters. Was this the motive of Paul as he wrote the Ephesian Christians in the middle of the first century? Did he state concrete and universal doctrine that segmented men and women within the church, delineating gender-specific dos and don'ts for worship and service? Or was Paul focusing totally and completely on the church of the first century that was struggling due to varied internal and external issues? Did Paul follow Jesus as the leading voice for rights and equality of women in the church and in society, or was he in reality misogynistic? We will explore these questions later in the session. First, though, we will study this difficult section that has polarized practice and discussion for centuries.

Men: How to Pray

Paul continues on the previous course with a practical instruction on the manner of prayers in public worship meetings. The early church met on a daily basis for worship, prayer, instruction, and food, as evidenced by Acts 2:42. "They devoted themselves," Luke reports, "to the apostles' teaching and fellowship, to the breaking of bread and prayers." The earliest fellowships celebrated Communion through the "agape feast," the same common fellowship meal Paul warned the Corinthians to honor with holy practices (1 Cor 11:17-34). It seems there were several abuses taking place in the Corinthian church concerning the daily gathering and Communion celebration that warranted Paul to teach from the negative. He takes a decidedly more muted approach in the Timothy letters, but nonetheless deals with certain behaviors within the worship experience. The early church was such an amalgamation of peoples that it should be no surprise that problems would ensue from their common gatherings, specifically from the joining together of Greek pagans and Hebrew traditionalists.

One aspect of specific instruction designed to provide order, structure, and equality to the worship experience was the manner of public prayer. Paul combined two aspects of the prayer act, one internal and the other external, to provide a common ground for disparate believers. He told them (men) "to lift up holy hands in prayer, without anger or disputing" (1 Tim 2:8). This command is symbolic of the ritual purification required of Hebrew men before prayer in the temple or synagogue. Second Chronicles 6:12 records Solomon praying before the altar: "Then he stood before the altar of the Lord in the presence of all the assembly of Israel and spread out his hands." Psalm 141:2 contains David's prayer for sanctification and protection: "May my prayer be counted as incense before Thee; the lifting up of my hands as the evening offering." This approach to praying would seem unusual to modern believers but was the common practice of Judaism and of the earliest Christians. To lift one's palm and face upward toward heaven was to seek God's blessing personally through supplication.

Paul then merged from highly symbolic to purely practical by citing the necessity of being internally clean before seeking God's blessing. According to John Calvin, "Paul uses the outward sign for the inward reality, for our hands indicate a pure heart" (214). This alleviates the obvious need to outstretch one's hands and rely on a set posture for effective praying. Paul was being neither overly Hebrew or legalistic in these words; rather, he was demonstrating the absolute requirement to be internally pure. In a church rife with controversies, bad theology, and argument, the act of prayer was no doubt also being compromised. The overtone is simply this: if a person approaches God with unconfessed sin, resentment, bitterness, or envy, God cannot work. Effective, genuine prayer must generate from an inward point of reverence and gratitude toward God, while at the same time not entertaining selfish drives or weak doubting. In the same vein, prayer should never be relegated to a perfunctory act done to appease God, "a piece of sacred pantomime," as Patrick Fairburn warns (122). "To lift up holy hands is to pray sincerely, in a way congruent with one's behavior, without hypocrisy, single-mindedly, with a pure heart focused upon the one thing needful—attentiveness to the will of God" (Oden, 92).

> To sum up, although holiness, love and peace should always accompany our prayers, yet whether we stand, sit, bow down, kneel or fall on our faces and whether our hands are lifted, spread, folded, clasped, clapping or waving are matters of little consequence. (Stott, 83)

A Woman's Place

In first-century Jewish practice, women were excluded from all but the most elementary levels of study and participation. The patriarchal structure of ancient Judaism had held strong well into the time of Jesus and later of Paul. Add to this the Greek-Gentile aversion to women joining in intellectual discussion with men, and it becomes easier to see the full scope of the issues pertaining to female partic-ipation in the Ephesus church. Paul pointedly allows for only men to pray in the worship experience, even going as far as requiring women to learn in silence and submission. This restrictive com-mand seems to contradict the letters he wrote to the church in Corinth, where he allowed women both to pray and prophesy.

Was Paul the advocate for a new faith that provided historic opportunity to women, or was he simply following suite with the ancient Hebrews and the contemporary Greeks? Judaism did not allow for women to worship in the innermost portions of the tem-ple, nor did it provide faith education to females on an equal scale with males. Gentile-Greek culture relegated cultured women to the home and disallowed them from intellectual discourse. In both his-torical Judaism and first-century Greek culture, women in general endured segregation and subordination. Is Paul demanding more of the same, or is he, along with Jesus Christ, leading the way to unprecedented rights for women of faith?

Much like beauty, the answers to these questions are in the eye of the beholder. It is easy to read the New Testament in a cursory manner and see Paul as being anti–female. This would be, however, the least trustworthy method of Scripture study. Honest Scripture study requires contextualization—the process of determining to whom the letter was written, why it was written, when it was writ-ten, and what the unique issues were at the time of the writing. Paul was a master of writing letters to congregations that dealt almost entirely with the issues and problems of the people of that time in that place. The Corinthian problems were every bit as unique to Corinth as the Galatian issues were to the Galatian church. When one considers the fact that Paul did not hold a future view for the church due to his belief in Christ's imminent return, a much clearer picture of Paul's theology emerges.

It is quite possible that Paul never intended for his teachings to take on universal and eternal priorities. Paul saw the church of his time up against the ticking clock of God's resolution for creation. Paul's overall message detailed the need for great haste in evangeliz-ing the world of the first-century church. Since women were historically excluded from religious study and practice, they were consequentially further behind most men in the early church. Paul did not command further restriction as much as he allowed them time to grow and effectively to "catch up." If women were placed in positions of leadership prematurely, they would have likely hindered the acute mission due to inexperience and unpreparedness. He provided women the most precious gift possible in commanding them equal access and full quality in the faith.

Church Health

There is little doubt that multiple factors played into the unique commands toward women in the Ephesus church. Paul was quite specific as to how women should dress and to their level of participation within the church setting. He commanded them to "dress modestly, with decency and propriety, not with braided hair or gold or pearls or expensive clothes, but with good deeds, appropriate for women who worship God. A woman should learn in quietness and submission . . . to not teach or have authority over a man, to be silent" (1 Tim 2:9-12). Historically, people have used these words to place restrictions upon women in the church; few, however, have contextualized them to determine why Paul spoke this way. It's one thing to take these verses completely at face value but quite another to delve deeply in order to determine why the verses speak restrictively toward women.

A complete study of the first-century church in Ephesus demonstrates the *whys* of Paul's tough stance on the women of the faith. Due to the lack of Hebrew opportunities afforded women to study and take part in worship events, those who accepted Christ came in woefully behind their male counterparts. They simply lacked the knowledge and experience necessary to be stationed on the same levels as Hebrew male converts. Along those lines, male Hebrew converts would be unaccustomed to female equality within the fellowship and would need time to adjust. It is also possible that certain women were so overjoyed with their newly found freedom that they were overreacting and overreaching within the church setting.

Possibly the biggest issue was the influx into the church of Greek women who were formerly associated with the various pagan deities in Ephesus. This would be especially true of the Diana cult, also known as Artemis, who was worshiped as the goddess of fertility and motherhood. The Temple of Diana was so elaborate and large that it was numbered as one of the Seven Wonders of the Ancient World. The Diana adherents held to the supremacy of females and predominantly featured female priests. Men could worship in the temple, but, other than eunuchs, they rarely held positions of leadership. As with other sensually based pagan religions of the first century, Diana followers saw sexual relations with cultic prostitutes as equal to union with a deity. To this end, 1,000 temple prostitutes served daily at the temple, and annual orgiastic festivals were held to celebrate the goddess. Suffice it to say that converts from this cult and others similar did not arrive in their new faith sufficiently equipped for public prayer, teaching, or leadership. There was a genuine learning curve for women of all types in the church of Ephesus, which is undoubtedly why Paul placed this level of restrictions.

Dress the Part

How would a first-century Christian female dress in order to exhibit Christian qualities and characteristics? Simply put, diametrically different from the cultural norm in Ephesus, especially considering the many followers of Diana. Verses 9-10 provide a veritable dress code for female believers covering both dress and hairstyles, and contrast the need for an inner beauty that is never overridden by outward adornments. Bailey and Constable write, "A Christian woman should be remarkable for her Christ-like behavior more than for her clothes, hairstyle and other externals that are of primary importance to many unbelievers" (464). Paul commands women in the church to dress with modesty, decency, and propriety, which combine to suggest that Ephesus was the Hollywood of its day. To show much of the body was likely in vogue for women of Ephesian cults since sexuality would have been seen as a virtue. Plus, due to Diana worship being a religion focused upon needs of women, sexuality would have also been an outlet for power. The cultured rich in Ephesus would not have been prone to dress scantily but would have been ostentatious in flaunting their wealth and position. The excessive braiding of hair allowed for a display of wealth and position through the placement of long pins topped by ornate gems or gold. Obviously, the same would hold true for expensive clothes as noted in verse 9, which would call attention to the outer exhibition of social place over the inner spiritual reality.

So, was Paul stating that looking good is improper for Christian women? Go plain and please God? No. Again, he was dealing with the unique issues facing the new community of faith in Ephesus. Expensive and sensual clothes, layers of jewelry, and over-the-top hairstyles were apparently more important to Ephesian women than their faith lives. The possibility of this mindset invading and taking root in the Christian church was quite real, and Paul wanted to shut it out. He was emphatic in his teaching that Christian women should be above the fray of the latest fashions and self-indulgent trends. In short, Paul's new motto for the Christian women of Ephesus was "be different and demonstrate that difference."

> Your beauty should not come from outward adornment, such as braided hair and the wearing of gold jewelry and fine clothes. Instead, it should be that of your inner-self, the unfading beauty of a gentle and quiet spirit, which is of great worth in God's sight. (1 Pet 3:3-4)

Be Silent

Paul had already expanded the religious rights of women by allowing them to take part in the full worship experience. By affirming their position as "teachable members" and providing them "equal rights" (Life Application Commentary, 938), he had both elevated and advanced the place of women in the faith community. That said, he was also pointed in his restrictions concerning women in this specific church. As has already been mentioned, it is almost certain that the female converts in Ephesus were seriously deficient in education and experience with no short-term potential for teaching and leadership. They were simply so far behind the men, especially Hebrew male converts, that their service would have retarded the progress of the church. This would be especially true for a church troubled by Gnosticism, the intellectually deep quasi-theology prevalent in Ephesus. These women were not yet savvy enough to deal with a theology based on the life and death of Christ, much less the intricacies of a Greek pagan religion.

Paul's instruction to the women was to enjoy the learning process by quietly participating, thus allowing the natural spiritual growth process to take place. The only way for this to work would be for women to voluntarily cooperate and settle for a lesser role and position. The implications of this are actually less about inequality than about the future of the church. If this church was to make it out of the first century intact, it would first need to grow spiritually, then excise the various bad theologies. Consequently, women had few positive options other than settling for spiritually subservient roles that did not allow for teaching or holding positions of authority. Their time to lead had simply not yet come.

The Question of Eve

The notion that women will be saved through childbearing (1 Tim 2:14) is easily one of the most difficult to interpret in all of Scripture. It is safe to say that the classic salvation verses leave Eve and childbearing out of the equation entirely. So what did Paul have in mind with Eve and "birthing babies" being linked to salvation? Actually, he is utilizing themes also found in his second letter to the Corinthian Christians: "I am afraid that just as Eve was deceived by the serpent's cunning, your minds may somehow be led astray from your sincere and pure devotion to Christ" (2 Cor 11:3). Of course, this doesn't offer any clarity, since church leaders for centuries have used these odd verses to restrict women from official service roles. Despite the reality that no one actually knows what Paul meant in either of these texts, Eve has nonetheless been implicated as history's first sinner and the prime accomplice to the fall of humankind. So much for "minding one's own business in Paradise when up walks a serpent . . . !"

Paul was either the first to pile on Eve, or he did not have a specific indictment of Eve in mind at all. The latter reasoning is not held in high esteem among conservative believers who routinely utilize Paul to justify their literalist doctrine. However, a broad and contextual study of Paul's writings demonstrates that he was not placing all of humanities' ills on either one woman or all women in general. In his letter to the church in Rome, he actually places primary blame on Adam, not Eve, as Adam was the only one privy to God's commands about the trees. Since Paul has been critical of both Adam and Eve, it seems best to stay away from endorsing any blanket condemnations of women as being especially gullible or spiritually inferior. Over the centuries, church leaders have used these assumptions to disqualify women from teaching Scripture. Such a view would certainly go against the totality of Paul's work and would also infringe on the teaching of Jesus. A better option for deciphering these troubling verses may be found in a combination of deeper theology and the utilization of gender roles.

Since the bulk of Paul's writings on gender roles center on function, it is possible that he is stating that women take the lead at the human level of providing life, and in the case of Mary, life that brought salvation. The Life Application Commentary cites the "design" (940) for women being to bring forth life, thus fulfilling God's purposes. William Barclay sees it similarly: "women will find life and salvation, not in attending meetings, and not in addressing meetings, but in motherhood, which is their crown" (79). Again, possibly the best take on this comes from John Stott, who takes these verses into a deeply theological arena: "That women will be saved through the birth of a Child, meaning the birth of Christ" (87). This unique view removes the focus from both Eve and womankind and places it on the one woman who obeyed God and opened the door for the redemption of all men and women. "If Mary had not given birth to the Christ child there would have been no salvation for anybody. No greater honor has ever been given to woman than in the calling of Mary to be the mother of the Savior of the world" (Stott, 88).

Life Lessons

True or False: Paul was anti-female and taught a theology of inequality of the sexes. Hopefully at this point his difficult writings have been contextualized and the rationale for his restrictions has become clear. Paul was not writing to restrict or curtail the involvement of women in the ministry of the church. Paul had an intense love for the church and God's kingdom and taught so that the church would progress and be greatly successful. To that end, women were not yet ready to be the leaders who would progress the movement. Due to centuries of being subordinated, they were not sufficiently prepared to contribute in the available forms of leadership. Certain women were behind due to lives lived in pagan, sensual religions that abused them in various ways. Other women served pagan deities that exalted females, but not in ways that were remotely holy. All factors combined cried out for a period of preparation for women who accepted Christ as Messiah and Lord. The absolute worst stance would have been for Paul to acquiesce and promote women to positions they were ill equipped to hold. It is sad that Paul has been vilified for his teaching regarding women when in reality he opened unprecedented avenues of equality and access for women in the church.

Paul also dictated an approach for males in worship that demanded a level of spiritual purity and selflessness that is sorely needed in today's church. The modern church is the result of a slow, traditional drift to a state where worship is defined almost exclusively as a corporate gathering. Biblically, especially in the letters of Paul, it is not the venue or size of the crowd that creates genuine worship; it is the internal intent. Possibly the best option for the modern church would be to focus more intently on the approach to personal worship and less on the issues of women in leadership. Proper prayer modes and intensely personal worship won't be as power laden or controversial as women in ministry, but they will certainly lead to a more spiritual environment. If it is true that Paul's chief aim was to lead the church to a level of spirituality that would result in transforming the entire world, the goal should be nothing less today and forever.

1. In what ways do these worship and prayer instructions align with Paul's command to "fight the good fight" in 1 Timothy 1:18-19?

_____

_____

_____

_____

_____

_____

2. Describe ways in which genuine prayer is affected by external issues in the lives of believers.

_____

_____

_____

_____

_____

3. List elements of individual purity that are necessary for genuine prayer and personal worship to occur.

_____

_____

_____

_____

_____

4. Describe ways in which the dress and overall presentation of women could be harmful to the cause of Christ.

_____

_____

_____

_____

_____

_____

5. List ways in which Paul's writings that restrict women in the church have been taken out of context.

_____

_____

_____

_____

_____

_____

6. Simply put, should women be allowed to serve in leadership positions in today's church? Explain your reasoning.

_____

_____

_____

_____

_____

_____

7. How do you understand the odd verses pertaining to Eve, childbirth, and salvation?

_____

_____

_____

_____

_____

_____

Men and Women in the Church

8. In what ways has Eve been unjustly or incorrectly maligned due to her mistake?

_____

_____

_____

_____

_____

_____

The Role of Minister

The themes of the first two chapters of Paul's first letter to Timothy concern doctrine and conduct in public worship. In the third chapter, Paul focuses entirely on the roles and functions of church leadership, primarily overseer and deacon. The New Testament also lists various other descriptive titles for leadership roles, including apostle, bishop, and elder. The preponderance of evidence demonstrates that most of these terms became interchangeable over time and the actual roles were similar.

The title "apostle" was initially used for those who had served with Jesus and select others like Paul. Over time the term came to apply to devout followers or church representatives. Paul also had a tendency to interchange these titles and roles, often within the same letter. Any person studying the Pastoral Epistles of Paul will be forced to deal with these positions and functions and view them through the lens of the modern church. While that is the easiest frame of reference from which to deal with the early leadership roles, it is not necessarily the most advantageous for today's reader. As it is said, "times have changed, and so have the needs and functions of the church."

At the time of Paul's letter the early church was still meeting in homes and membership was quite small in number. Paul or his emissary would do the majority of teaching in each fellowship. The sheer transient nature of Paul's ministry, however, forced the young church to face up to local leadership issues. Neither Timothy nor Titus would have been expected to remain in these cities for the rest of their lives. Paul had sent both on missions before their time in Ephesus and Crete respectively, and chances were they would serve elsewhere in the future. All of this made it imperative for the church to elect people to serve and lead the believers in the case of either apostle being sent to a new locale by Paul. His focus in chapter 3 is thus preparatory for life without Timothy or, in the case of Crete, Titus. However, since it is clear that Paul wrote to the early church in specific locations, what should the modern church do with this chapter? Is the framework put into place for early church leadership still applicable or even feasible for today's uniquely different church? Is it possible to follow a process and plan that is now almost 2,000 years old?

Again, these are questions one cannot answer with total and complete certainty. As is the case with virtually all difficult areas of Scripture, the opinions are numerous and varied. One thing is for certain: the Timothy and Titus letters require more than a cursory, surface read and instant application with no questions asked in the process. This chapter has been used for eons to justify certain people being allowed in leadership roles and, subsequently, others being disqualified. Plus, consider the differences between the house-meeting church of Ephesus and Crete versus the church of today. Do you think Paul ever envisioned the Roman Catholic Church or the Southern Baptist Convention? Obviously not, especially since Paul viewed the church as having a rapidly approaching shelf life due to the "any day now" return of Christ. Possibly the best question concerns the ability to reconcile the two church eras in the first place. Can the church of today utilize a leadership framework borne out of a house church in Greece in the third quarter of the first century?

The best possible resolution would be to use the first-century Ephesian and Cretan models tempered by the realities of the modern church. Scripture does not offer a great deal of options in this matter, so whenever doctrine, theology, and practice come together on this subject, the words of Paul must be both applied and contextualized. The biggest issue for today's church has less to do with gender roles or marital history than it does with literality. This is where the 2,000 years of church history assist the process of application. The church has massively changed, but for many, the theological rendering of Paul's instructions has remained fixed in time. Ironically, much of the language and structure Paul used was already in place in the Greco-Roman world or had historical significance in Judaism. *Elder* is the oldest office to be found in Scripture. Every Hebrew synagogue had elders from the time when Moses appointed seventy men to assist with the control and care of the people of Israel (Num 11:16). The Spartans had a group of leaders translated *the board of elder men*. Rome's Parliament was called the Senate, which comes from the Latin word *senex,* meaning *an old man.* The British/English term *alderman* originally meant *elder men* (Barclay, 81). So Paul was not breaking completely new ground in his instructions to the church. He took historical and contemporary structures and adapted them to the new church. He tailored a system to meet the needs of a new and different religious order. He contextualized the language and structures of his day to benefit the church of his day. There is a great deal of positive truth to be learned from these chapters, as well as an opportunity to contemporize the theology and doctrine of church service.

Overseer

Paul begins with the role of overseer of the local church. The church in both Ephesus and Crete battled invasive elements of bad and divisive teaching that tore at the foundation of its fellowship. Some of these erroneous teachers also lived immoral lives, and coupled with the overall moral climate of Greece and the Roman Empire, models of purity and honor were sorely needed within the church. This is one of the reasons Paul established the role of overseer, the person charged with leading and modeling genuine faith for the believers. Before setting qualifications for leadership selection, he established that the office of overseer is "a noble task," and "anyone who sets their heart on being an overseer" (1 Tim 3:1) aspires to a noble calling. It should be noted that Paul was not saying anyone who desires to be a church leader should become one. Nothing could be farther from the inferred truth of these verses. In Acts 20:28, he states, "Keep watch over yourselves and all the flock of which the Holy Spirit has made you overseers." God specifically calls forth those who will pastor and shepherd the fellowship of believers. To be called to a noble task such as this is a setting apart for ministry. The responsibility of the church is to screen those who feel called to lead in ministry, effectively applying a set of prescribed criteria onto the life of a candidate.

The first qualification is to be *above reproach.* Paul states that the overseer must be of good reputation and "have no flaw in conduct that would be grounds for any kind of accusation" (Life Application Commentary, 941). Thomas Oden adds, "one's conduct would give no opportunity to critics to injure the church, as detractors will search diligently to find fault in leaders" (141).

Obviously this statement does not infer a lack of sin. The intent is to establish that no serial sin pattern is present that would do harm to the church.

The next qualification listed is *the husband of one wife.* There is little doubt that this single criterion has elicited more discussion and scrutiny than all other qualifications combined. The possible interpretations of this statement are long and varied. However, since no one knows exactly what Paul meant by the statement, it is best to give study to each genuine possibility. It is possible Paul was speaking against the practice of polygamy with this qualification. While it is true that polygamy was not a massive problem for the early church, the practice of having more than one wife at one time was practiced by Jews of that era. Justin Martyr, second-century theologian, wrote of "imprudent and blind Jewish teachers who even till this time permit each man to have four or five wives" (Stott, 93). Pagan Greeks also practiced it, meaning the arrangement could easily find its way into the church with the conversion of Gentiles. John Calvin adapts the views of early theologian Chrysostom, definitively stating that Paul is arguing against the polygamy practiced by some Hebrews who cited Abraham and David as having multiple wives and against the rampant immoral marital practices of the Greeks (54).

Another popular interpretation is that Paul was arguing against remarriage after divorce. It is true that Jesus "raised the bar" for the sanctity of marriage by asserting that one simply should not divorce. Jesus was not being an "activist" with this blanket prohibition against divorce; he was being a "reactivist" against the loose divorce habits of Jews. It was amazingly easy for a Jewish man to divorce his wife; in fact, it had become an epidemic of selfish pursuits in which older Jewish men were trading in longtime wives for new, younger spouses. Ephesus was also a well-traveled port city and a hub for pagan religions that focused on sensual spirituality. To be sexually selfish was common to both the culture and the temple, thus the norms and mores were well established. Since immorality and divorce were equally common in the Greco-Roman world, Paul would have been on guard to make certain that the loose societal views would not infiltrate the leadership ranks of the church.

The resulting question concerns the sequence of the marital injunction: was the focus divorce or remarriage after divorce? It would be easier to make a case for prohibiting remarriage if one takes into account Paul's writing in 1 Corinthians 7, but even there he allows for the divorce of a couple where one spouse is an unbeliever. It was also commonly held that the believing spouse was free to marry again without penalty. Suffice it to say that the church is yet again faced with an issue of tremendous importance without any level of certainty as to what Paul had in mind.

The final common view concerns marital fidelity. An exhaustive review of commentary literature on Paul's teaching on this verse suggests that this is the majority view of scholars and theologians. If this is the case, Paul was advocating the one-man-one-woman approach to relationships. A proper translation of this verse would be "a one-woman man," signifying a commitment to high morals and to marriage. George Knight comments on the overseer's morals: "A man who having contracted a monogamous marriage is faithful to his marriage vows" (158-59). Stott agrees that fidelity in marriage is what Paul had in mind: "This explanation seems to fit the context best here. The accredited overseers of the church, who are called to teach doctrine and exercise discipline, must themselves have an unblemished reputation in the area of sex and marriage" (94). In a society and climate of rampant immorality centered on adultery, fornication, homosexuality, and divorce, Paul was advocating a strict code of behavior that would clearly define the difference between church and society.

The next three qualifications are routinely grouped together: *temperate, self-controlled,* and *respectable. Temperate* is the positive form of intemperate and often means to use wisdom concerning alcohol. John Calvin defines this as "avoiding intemperance in guzzling" (90), which in common speak would mean not to get drunk, or at least not to drink really fast! Other possibilities are to be soberminded, which would concern judgment and not alcohol. *Self-controlled* is the easiest to define and basically means to exercise good judgment in all situations. Not to "lose control" would be a way for the church leader to be a positive witness and example. There was a classic Greek thought that self-control was the safeguard of the most excellent habits in life. A more modern approach links *self-control* and *respectable* together as parallel inward and outward expressions. By being in control, one will display respectability in all situations, thus providing a positive witness for the faith. Paul instructs Timothy to "run the race" but also within the "rules" (2 Tim 2:5). Again, self-control and a selfless mindset are required for ministry leadership. Sixteenth-century French writer Francois

Rabelias asks, "How shall I be able to rule over others if I have not full power and command of myself?" (Frame, 52).

The next qualification is more specific to the role of professional overseer. To be *able to teach* is to have the ability to understand and communicate the truths of Scripture and to assist in their application. In both Crete and Ephesus, the overseer would also require the ability to determine and oppose false teaching. This would necessitate a mature faith and the spiritual gift of teaching, which together would equip the person to present doctrine and theology effectively.

In 1 Timothy 3:3, Paul lists characteristics to be avoided in the church leader: *not a drunkard, not violent but gentle, not quarrelsome and not a lover of money.* Greek culture in general was open to the free flow of wine and, apparently from all New Testament sources, the church never reacted against alcohol in moderation. Paul even instructed Timothy to substitute wine for the water he was drinking for his stomach ailment (1 Tim 5:23). Since the teaching was to use wine with restraint, it is not surprising that the overseer was instructed not to overindulge. Temperance and self-control were required of the church leader, not only with alcohol but also in demeanor. The overseer was not to be a divisive, violent, or argumentative person. No doubt the false teachers were using the patented practice of intellectual debate, which is little more than organized argument, and the church was fragmenting as a result. In a society where no absolute truth existed, the church would be a haven for the security of absolute and eternal faith realities. The overseer was charged with maintaining the sanctity of church by minimizing division and proclaiming genuine truth.

It was also of paramount importance for the overseer not to place inordinate attention on money. Since the love of money is deemed the root of all evil (1 Tim 6:10), the overseer would be living in a state of serial sin if money were the driving force of life. Ethical handling of church monies would be a part of the job for overseers, so trust would be a necessity. Plus, many of the itinerant philosophers saw teaching as enterprise and made a business of it. Consequently, the overseer would need to be above the lure and temptation of money and material gain to model and lead effectively.

Paul's next qualifier concerns the family of the overseer: *He must manage his own family well and see that his children obey him with respect* (1 Tim 3:4). With this verse, Paul contrasts the proper management of the family with that of the church. The following verse adds, "If anyone does not know how to manage his own family, how can he take care of God's church?" The Life Application Commentary defines the translation of *manage* as "compassionate governing, leading and directing, not stern, cruel, tyrannical, and authoritarian dominance" (942). This depicts a leadership style built on love and not fear. Respect is earned through leadership that is consistent, positive, and love-based. Just as morality cannot be legislated, neither can respect. These qualities must be transferable from the home to the church and vice-versa.

Paul also deems *recent converts*, or new believers, as not being qualified for leadership of the church. This restriction makes a great deal of sense to today's reader but would have met with some resistance among early believers. Picture the makeup of the first-century church at the time of Paul's writing to Timothy. It would have been made up of mainly new converts, especially among the majority Gentiles. This fact would have severely diminished the number of candidates for overseer and deacon. However, the rhyme and reason for Paul's injunction is readily understandable. New converts had not yet been sufficiently grounded in the faith to assume positions of leadership. The learning curve for new believers in general would have been steep, but this would have been especially true for converts from the pagan Greek religions.

Life Lessons

Paul seemed to hold no future view of the Christian church due to his steadfast belief in the imminent return of Christ. Despite this common view of the early church, the movement did indeed progress out of the first century and has endured for almost 2,000 years. While there are many factors involved in this magnificent progression and expansion, pastoral leadership would have to be rated near the top of any list.

It is commonly held that no body of believers is able to mature beyond the level of its primary leader. If this is correct, then the need for proper leadership cannot be overstated, nor can it be overcome through structure and style. God has ordained the process and qualifications for pastoral leadership, and through Paul's concise instructions the church has a framework for assessing and calling ministry candidates. Sadly, the tendency has been to take a literal rendering of this section. While each church is biblically unique and should function autonomously, this freedom can be taken too far.

Genuine abuse takes place when a church selectively interprets these instructions for the purposes of exclusion from ministry. When this occurs, the church automatically defaults to a process that is incongruent with the modern church. To be honest to Scripture and to the intent of the initial writing, each of these qualifications should be properly interpreted, contextualized, and applied. John Stott laments the lowered standards accepted by the modern church over its first-century counterpart:

> Although some commentators disparage these ten qualifications for the pastorate as pedestrian, and as suitable for secular leadership, they have far reaching Christian implications. And if Paul's standards are regarded by some as comparatively low, we need to reflect that contemporary standards are lower still! For the selection procedure of many churches today does not include an examination of candidates in these ten areas. They constitute a necessary, comprehensive and challenging test. (99)

This dilemma is made even worse if the church process focuses exclusively on the "big two" of gender and divorce. Properly interpreted and properly applied, the twenty-first-century church has a biblical framework for defining and selecting church leadership in the Pastoral Epistles. There is no need to reinvent the wheel yet again in this arena.

1. In what ways would the desire to be in ministry be positive? Conversely, in what ways might this desire be negative?

_____

_____

_____

_____

_____

_____

2. What does Paul mean by the minister being "above reproach"?

_____

_____

_____

3. Explain all possible meanings of "husband of one wife."

_____

_____

_____

_____

_____

_____

4. If "husband of one wife" were placed in the context of the modern church, how might it best be applied?

_____

_____

_____

_____

_____

_____

5. In what ways does this text open the way for women in ministry?

_____

_____

_____

_____

_____

_____

6. In what ways does this text preclude women from ministry?

_____

_____

_____

_____

_____

7. Why should a church view the entire ministry family in the process of calling the minister?

_____

_____

_____

_____

_____

_____

8. How would being in love with money and material wealth be problematic for the minister?

_____

_____

_____

_____

_____

_____

9. Paul cautions against electing new converts to ministry positions. Why is this still a good practice for the modern church?

_____

_____

_____

_____

_____

_____

10. Why should the modern church pay attention to all the qualifications Paul lists?

_____

_____

_____

_____

_____

_____

The Role of Deacon

Session

1 Timothy 3:8-13

Paul continues his teaching on intra-church leadership by citing qualifications for the role of deacon. Oddly, there is no set teaching in the New Testament that defines or delineates the exact duties of the deacon, nor is there a history of when, or even why, deacons came into existence. It is widely accepted that the role of deacon did exist in the early church before Paul's writing to Timothy, possibly beginning with the pronounced needs of widows as described in Acts 6:1-4:

> In those days when the number of disciples was increasing, the Grecian Jews among them complained against those of the Aramaic-speaking community because their widows were being overlooked in the daily distribution of food. So the Twelve gathered all the disciples together and said, "It would not be right for us to neglect the ministry of the Word of God in order to wait on tables. Brothers, choose seven men from among you who are known to be full of the Spirit and wisdom. We will turn this responsibility over to them and will give our attention to prayer and the ministry of the word."

It should be noted that those chosen for service in the Jerusalem church were not called "deacons." Paul had a tendency to use the Greek word translated *deacon* for anyone who served the kingdom, including himself (Phil 1:1). He includes the word in Romans 12:7 as a needed spiritual gift and models it personally by taking up money for the drought- and famine-stricken Jerusalem believers in 2 Corinthians 8:1-15. There is little doubt that early believers would have easily recognized the role of deacon by the longstanding meaning of the basic Greek word. *Diakonos* essentially signified servant, with a specific first-century meaning of "waiter at table." This definition was initially used to identify the character of the servant rather than form a job description of the official church role. The absolute specifics of what a deacon was to do continued to be sketchy throughout Scripture. The qualifications, however, became more and more specific and well known as the church continued to develop. This disconnect between qualifications versus role most likely did not have any adverse consequences for the early church in Ephesus. To understand *diakonos* as *servant* was to understand the subsidiary role of one who served the needy. The beauty of this self-defined flexibility undoubtedly allowed for many variations of the role from one church to the next as the first-century church progressed.

The bulk of Hebrew history also assisted the new role of deacon in becoming more established in role and function. William Barclay best details the historical social practices of the Jews that led to blanket care for the poor and disadvantaged. The synagogue created an organization for helping people of need in a unified, cooperative sense. An individual providing for the poor and hungry was frowned upon in each Hebrew community, with the preferred model being a collective support approach. Each Friday two collectors would go door to door to collect money and items from businesses and homes in order to provide for the disadvantaged. The collected monies and items were pooled together and distributed by a select committee. The poor were given enough food for two meals per day for fourteen days, unless a family already had food supplies for seven days. If that were the case, they were skipped on that round of distribution. The committee also administered a collection and distribution plan for emergency needs. This approach was shifted into the early Christian church model and allowed for deacons to be both collector and distribution committee (98).

The Christian church clearly delineated two categories of leaders—overseers and deacons. Overseer, elder, and bishop were for the most part interchangeable until the early second century and were the teacher-leader of the church. Philippians 1:1 cites both leader groups: "To all the saints in Christ Jesus in Philippi, together with the overseers and deacons." Overseers led all early churches, with the establishing evangelist filling the role until the church was strong enough to be led by another person. Often the establishing overseer would select the successor, which is a practice Paul used in most cases, and if not, the church would select from within. In the case of deacon, however, not every church selected and installed servant leaders. In church bodies that did not utilize deacons, the overseer had a great deal more responsibility. Clearly, the model demonstrated in Acts 6, accompanied by the qualifications found in the Timothy letters, was the best distribution of resources for the ministry-minded early church. In contrast to the Hebrew synagogue, the Christian church balanced social ministry with evangelism, requiring much more from servant leaders. If the Hebrew practices were one-dimensional, the early New Testament church was truly multi-dimensional.

Over time the role of deacon evolved into a greatly different model from what the early church practiced. By the second century, the deacon role was an established one in all churches. From that point forward it has morphed into the modern version that hardly resembles the original in any form. However, that can be said for virtually all aspects of the church, so this should not be seen as an indictment of modern leadership. Possibly the best way to view progress in deacon ministry over time is to grade today's practice with the original intent of the role. If service and base ministry is foundational to today's deacon ministry, the original intent has remained true for almost 2,000 years. On the other hand, if the deacon ministry has become primarily a ruling body that "runs" the business of the church, the original intent has been replaced by a modern reaction. One has to admit that modern deacons should be in the know and, at times, decision makers. If, however, that role is the sole deacon function, a generous break with the New Testament intent has occurred.

Qualifications for Deacons

Paul lists qualifications of deacons in 1 Timothy 3:8-13, leading with *worthy of respect*. Many versions have "men" leading the sentence, but "men" is not actually in the Greek text. Translators added it as an assumption of implication. The modern view of a leader who "commands respect" is quite foreign to Paul's description in this verse. Respect should not be automatically garnered due to position alone. Respect must be earned by life practice and modeling of righteous behavior. "Worthy" is a key descriptive word in this qualification. Worth signifies some level of attainment, and as such, respect may be earned after an outward expression of proper living. Due to the complexities of translating multiple-meaning Greek words into English, "respect" has more meanings in Greek than in

English. The classic definition would be one of reciprocity, where a person is not only one who receives respect, but one who supplies it as well. In Paul's time, respect was first given and then received. The same Greek word was used in 1 Timothy 2:4, "quiet lives in all godliness and holiness," and suggests a person of dignity and integrity based on Christ's model.

Sincere is the next qualification of the deacon and signifies a person who "is not double-tongued" (NSRV). A related modern colloquial phrase is "not speaking out of both sides of the mouth." A deacon is always to model Christ in speech and communication. Some have viewed this as simply not gossiping, but in reality it means much more. The totality of a deacon's speech habits must be above board and overtly Christian, thus not being open to the charge of hypocrisy. Ralph Earle, in *Word Meanings in the New Testament*, defines this as "not having the intent to deceive" (391). Once again, integrity is to be part of a deacon's speech practices.

The next qualifier is *not indulging in much wine.* Just as the overseer was not to have overindulgence issues with wine and strong drink, neither must the deacon. To have problems with wine would signify a lack of self-control on the part of the deacon. This would indicate poor judgment as well, and possibly jeopardize how he or she might treat other people or property. It is a historically accurate statement that virtually all people drank wine in the first-century Greco-Roman world (with the exception of Hebrew and pagan priests in respective temple ceremonies). While the Christian deacon was not excluded from drinking alcohol, he or she was to exercise great judgment when doing so.

Paul also taught that deacons *should not pursue dishonest gain.* One version reads, "Greedy of filthy lucre," but since the word "lucre" isn't used much anymore, the idea of dishonest gain best covers the prohibition. This is all one word in Greek and occurs only in the New Testament here and in Titus 1:7, where it refers to a bishop. Obviously Paul had a single focus in the Timothy and Titus letters on integrity in all areas for church leaders. It is quite possible that deacons would be in charge of church funds, especially if they served in ways similar to those in Jerusalem. Since money has always been a delicate subject to those in the church, financial sanity and smart practice was imperative for the deacon.

In verse 9, Paul cites the need for deacons to *keep hold of the deep truths of the faith with a clear conscience.* The NSRV reads, *they must hold fast to the mystery of the faith with a clear conscience.* In New

Testament language, *mystery* does not hold the same meaning as the common English term today. Rather than mysterious, cryptic, or unfathomable, the Greek word denotes something "once hidden which has been discovered and made known by revelation from God" (Hovey, 42). This was uniquely necessary in the pagan-infested city of Ephesus, especially with the inherent problem of false teachers within the church. In 1 Timothy 1:19, Paul speaks of false teachers who have rejected their conscience and damaged their faith. In essence, they missed the entire point of faith in Christ. It was never to be a rational exercise led by a rational spiritual leader teaching a variation of existing truths. It was God delivering the message of salvation in a heretofore unknown mode that came with but one requirement: faith.

British pastor and author Tom Wright writes, "'Do not be conformed to this world, but be transformed'; in other words, don't let the pagan world shape your worldview, your praxis, your symbolic universe, your thinking" (143). In Acts 6:13, the seven people chosen are "known to be full of the Spirit and wisdom." While these early servants were not referred to as deacons, they served as vicarious models of what deacon servants should embody. First and foremost, the deacon must be a person filled with the Holy Spirit and one in touch with the foundational truths of Christianity. The Life Application Commentary defines the "*mystery* or *deep truths* as the plan of salvation now fully known in Christ (Rom. 16:26; 1 Cor. 2:7, 4:1; Eph. 3:3-9; Col. 1:26). Originally unknown to humanity, this plan became crystal clear when Jesus rose from the dead" (67).

Paul also commands deacon candidates *first be tested, then if there is nothing against them, let them serve as deacons.* The New English Bible reads, "undergo a scrutiny," which suggests the entire church would engage in the process of evaluating the totality of the candidate's worthiness. Stott sees this as a "period of probation in which the congregation may assess the character, beliefs and gifts of the deacon candidate" (101). This rigorous process would have been especially important in the first century due to the volume of immigrants into the new faith from disparate backgrounds. It would be hard to argue against such a structure and fashion in today's church as well, especially considering the odd variety of methods in use for selecting deacons in the modern church.

The next section of qualifications is easily the most volatile for the modern church both to decipher and apply. Sadly, this has not stopped many churches from ignoring any and all levels of difficulty and opting for the easy, literal reading of verse 11. Easy, however, does not always mean correct or historically accurate, and literal always has a margin for error when taking Scripture from Greek to English. This is especially true when the biases of translators become additions to the text, which has happened numerous times in 1 Timothy 3:11. The New International Version reads, *In the same way their wives are to be women worthy of respect, not malicious talkers but temperate and trustworthy in everything.* Simple, right? Case closed. Deacons who have wives are males, so putting two and two together provides the orthodox answer for selecting deacons— Males Only, Females Need Not Apply! The biggest problem with this literal interpretation is the tedious fact that *their* is not in the original Greek sentence. Also, the word Paul used (*gynaikes*) is a rather ordinary word for both *women* and *wives*. The Revised Standard Version uses "Women in like manner," while the New Revised Standard Version opts for "Women likewise"—both of which signify the majority usage of the Greek word most common for a female.

In reality, this verse could refer to the wives of deacons, to deaconesses, to female deacons, or just to women. While the odds favor simply *women*, the argument must be augmented with other components in order to make the strongest case possible for Paul's meaning. Possibly the other significant fact is where he places this statement. It must not be lost on the modern reader that this segment is in the middle of his overall teaching on deacon qualifications. With the original language almost certainly favoring *women* over *wives*, and with Paul citing qualifiers for both women and men for deacon ministry, the role should be one open for qualified *people* regardless of gender. Yet another indicator is the fact that Paul does not list qualifications for wives of overseers. If the wife of the lead overseer did not merit qualifications, why would the wife of a secondary leader need to meet specific criteria? Plus, why would a qualification be necessary in the first place if the wife or spouse were not elected to a role of service?

One could easily ask why Paul did not make all of this easier by simply citing *deaconesses* in verse 11 rather than the somewhat troublesome *wives* or *women*. Actually, he did not have a choice, as the Greek language did not have a separate word at that time for "deaconess"; *diakonos* was a one-size-fits-all term for both male and female deacons. An additional support for female deacons in this verse is Paul laying down stringent qualifiers for the women. Just as he did specifically for men, Paul charged the Ephesus church to hold women deacon candidates to high, ethical standards. His specific instruction concerning female deacons states that they *must be worthy of respect, not malicious talkers but temperate and trustworthy in everything.* Women servants must exhibit the same hallmarks of integrity as their male counterparts. In addition, they specifically should not slander or gossip, they must show moderation and self-control in all things, and they should faithfully discharge their duties in and for the church. If one considers the references to Phoebe of Cenchreae (Rom 16:1), Euodia and Synyche (Phil 4:2), Tabitha (Acts 9:36-41), and others mentioned, the case is made for female deacons serving during the formative years of the church.

Paul's final qualification for the deacon candidate states, *a deacon must be the husband of one wife and must manage his children and his household well.* The easiest deduction here would be the prohibition against divorce, but just as with the case of overseer qualifications, no one really knows what Paul had in mind. It could mean that Paul prohibits anyone who has divorced a spouse from serving as deacon, or it could apply to remarriage after divorce, or it could prohibit the practice of polygamy. Any and all of these were issues affecting the early church, and each is covered in Scripture at some level. Thus, all are active possibilities. Theologian Wayne Grudem leans heavily toward polygamy being the focus of this verse:

> A better interpretation is that Paul was prohibiting a polygamist (a man who *presently* has more than one wife) from serving. All the other qualifications refer to a man's *present status*, not his entire past life. In I Timothy 3:1-7 it does not mean "one who has *never been* a lover of money," but "one who is *not now* a lover of money." It does not mean "one who has been above reproach for his whole life," but "one who is now above reproach." If we made these qualifications apply to one's past life, then we would exclude from office almost everyone who became a Christian as an adult. Paul could have said, "having been married only once" if he had wanted to, but he did not. (917)

Obviously this view does not answer all questions relating to marital status or history of deacon candidates, but it does assist in widening the debate. It is far too easy to take yet another literal reading of these verses and stake out a dogmatic theological and doctrinal stance for deacon qualifications. This cursory approach would ignore the contextual and language issues constantly in play when breaking down Paul's letters. Since no one knows exactly what Paul had in mind for the Ephesus church, it would seem that dogmatism would not be a legitimate, even ethical option.

Deacon Candidates in a Nutshell

To cite specific duties for a deacon in the New Testament would be difficult. Possibly the best description of "deaconing" is found in Acts 6, despite the fact that the seven people chosen to serve were not called deacons. In this case, seven people were chosen to serve the unique and expanding needs of the Jerusalem church. To make matters even more complicated, the only specific reference to a deacon in a church setting in the New Testament is Phoebe, who, incidentally, was female. It is no wonder that today's practices and processes are all over the proverbial board with little similarities existing across denominational lines. Scripture teaches us that deacons are first and foremost servants who actively serve other people and, subsequently, the church itself. One must meet certain qualifications, but the specifics listed by Paul must never be read in a cursory or trivial manner. These verses require more than a literal glance and instant dogma. To honor this ministry role properly, a church would need to attend to these verses through deep study and even deeper prayer.

Life Lessons

It would be safe to admit that few church roles, structures, and functions present today resemble those of the early church. This reality would definitely be the case when viewing the biblical format for deacon, as we are provided much more in the way of qualifications than in direct function. What ministry description we do have, however, demonstrates that the early deacon was exclusively one who served the people. This fact makes a great deal of sense after considering that Paul charged the overseer (pastor/minister/teacher) with overall leadership, and clearly demonstrated that these two distinct roles were both necessary and complimentary. In order for the overseer to evangelize and teach adequately, the deacons were to take care of the day-to-day needs of the people, specifically orphans, widows, and the poor. The early church became the social safety net for those who were marginalized or who had no hope for survival otherwise. The deacons, in effect, modeled the gospel through direct ministries and assisted the over-seer in "proving" the gospel message genuine. It was the almost perfect blending together of words and actions that combined to demonstrate and explain God's plans through the church.

It certainly seems correct that today's approach to deacon min-istry morphed along the historical time line and now resembles more an oversight committee than a ministry outlet. It would be difficult to pinpoint the beginning of the drift, but it likely began at about the same point that the modern church lost its prime position of influencing society. Few would argue the fact that we live in a "post-church" age, a time in which the church is closer to historical artifact than the agent of "salt and light" Jesus commanded. It is arguable but possible that the demise is the result of losing the min-istry of deacon to a perceived need for oversight and leadership. Possibly a return to the biblical roots of pure service is an answer to the decline of the institution. If so, Paul's incomplete instructions on the role of deacon serve as a jumping-off point for reclaiming the deacon servant. Paul was more than thorough in the qualifications for deacon, and it would undoubtedly serve the church well to take *all* items on the list seriously when selecting for the office. It is also imperative fully and adequately to contextualize Paul's words to Ephesus and Crete and not fall prey to the easy, literal read that automatically disqualifies segments of the church from service.

In the proper context of the status of women in the Greco-Roman world and the often troublesome translational issues, we can readily see that Paul wrote to these specific churches at these specific times with these specific instructions. Did Paul entertain the notion that we would be dealing with questions related to deacon ministry almost 2,000 years later? It is highly unlikely that he did, so to do justice to his writings we have no choice but to contextualize them before application. This should open doors to the possibility of women in deacon ministry and, at the very least, allow for discus-sion on the actual meaning of "husband of one wife." To be willing to contextualize these verses is to be willing to be honest with Scripture as it was written. Anything short of this is simply selective reading and interpreting to suit either the status quo or personal preference. Even if little changes as a result of the contextualization process, due diligence would have taken place. The office of deacon alone is worthy of such openness to the possibilities of Scripture.

The Role of Deacon

1. In what ways has deacon ministry remained the same over the millennia?

_____

_____

_____

_____

_____

_____

2. In what ways did Paul contextualize the existing Jewish practices in explaining the role of deacon?

_____

_____

_____

_____

_____

_____

3. In your view, which qualifications are the most important for today's deacon candidate? Explain.

_____

_____

_____

_____

_____

_____

4. Cite possible negatives resulting from a deacon who is also a lover of money.

_____

_____

_____

_____

_____

5. Should the modern deacon abstain from alcohol or simply not overindulge? Explain.

_____
_____
_____
_____
_____
_____

6. Make a case for female deacons from these sections by Paul.

_____
_____
_____
_____
_____

7. Conversely, make a case for the prohibition of female deacons from these same sections.

_____
_____
_____
_____
_____

8. Should the family of a deacon candidate be scrutinized in the selection process? Explain.

_____
_____
_____
_____
_____

9. In what ways do divorce issues pertain to the selection and qualification of deacons?

_____

_____

_____

_____

_____

_____

In the Last Days

Paul was the greatest church planter and evangelist in all of Christian history. He had great love for the church, placing it as primary to reaching the Greco-Roman world in the name of Christ. To that end, he established the church as belonging to "the living God" and functioning as "the pillar and foundation of the truth" (1 Tim 3:15). He also established that the church is no longer corporate in nature, as evidenced in the long history of the Hebrews, but individual and inclusive of all who profess Jesus as Lord. As the custodian and living witness of the truth of the gospel, the church could not "contain" and thus discriminately distribute the truth. The truth was, and is, much larger than the church. As the Life Application Commentary states, "the truth would still exist if there were no churches; the truth would still exist whether anyone believed it or not" (71). Paul commanded Timothy to live this truth, to teach it, to preach it, and to guard it against all malevolent forces. Paul made this case in his usual abstract way, shifting from the role of the church to additional teaching on the malevolent forces threatening the new movement.

Paul dedicated a great deal of space in the Pastoral Epistles to the dangers of false teachers, essentially employing repetitive cycles of focus every few chapters. For the first time in the Timothy and Titus letters, he links false doctrine with the "later times" (1 Tim 4:1). Paul began the initial letter to Timothy with issues related to false teaching, indicating the pernicious nature of the problems facing the Ephesus church. In both the Galatian and Corinthian writings, he coined a unique term citing this contrary teaching as a "different gospel" that taught both a "different Jesus" and a "different Spirit" (2 Cor 11:1). The first- and second-century church saw a continuing expression of contrary teaching that mixed portions of classic Judaism with outside pagan and philosophical notions, combining to alter the primacy of Jesus. A short, simple barometer of what constitutes false theology is determined by the orthodoxy test of the divinity and deity of Jesus. If a system of belief denies any aspect of Jesus as God, then it is purely bad theology and an affront to the orthodox teachings of the New Testament. In today's world the church battles cultic teachings that routinely alter the divinity of Jesus. Due to 2,000 years of experience and sophisticated theological study, it is now quite easy to identify and counter aberrant theology. Neither Timothy nor Titus were as fortunate, however, as contrary voices were prevalent and easily meshed into the early fellowship of new believers. If the enemies of today's church operate in the backdrop of "black and white," the early church faced the "full spectrum of gray" in its pivotal beginnings. As insidious as these voices were, Paul's biggest problem had more to do with the imminent return of Christ than all false teachers combined. He saw the clock ticking and little time remaining to take the gospel to the entire known world. While false teachers in the midst were slowing progress, the biggest enemy for Paul was time itself.

As has been stated over and again, Paul had no future view for the church. He believed Jesus would return at any moment and that the church would endure only for a short amount of time. For Paul, God's plans would be fulfilled within his generation. Obviously, Jesus did not return according to the early church timetable, and Paul was, in a word, wrong. This fact alone has done more to shape the evolving theology and mindset of the church than any other theological issue, including false theology. As later New Testament books were written, this disappointing reality became evident.

After AD 70, however, with the destruction of the temple in Jerusalem and the realization that the church was entering into a second (and in some cases even a third) generation, it became clear that Jesus was not going to return within the originally expected time period. The truth was an embarrassment to these people and caused many to rethink the issue. In fact, almost all of the New Testament books written after AD 70 deal in some way with the disappointment and embarrassment over the delay of the Parousia. Chronologically, the letter known as 2 Peter is the last of the canonical New Testament writings. The author explains that there has been a delay, but God will bring the world to an end when God decides to do so. No timetable is set! (Efird, 7)

We continue to exist today as the church built on the eventual return of Christ. No part of our theology can remain intact if that belief is forfeited, so we labor on toward that end. We must also resist the temptation to involve ourselves in God's decision-making process, in effect assisting with the planning. It is simply not our place to determine when God will act finally and decisively. If Paul was flawed in his assessments, who are we to take up the mantle of supreme prophecy? This hasn't stopped many from doing just that, however, as history has been rife with failed determinations of the return of Jesus. In 1998 a booklet appeared that cited ninety-eight reasons why Jesus would return that particular year. The following year, it was republished with one additional reason, seriously damaging the author's credibility in both theology and prognostication. Add in *The Late, Great Planet Earth* by Hal Lindsay and the more recent *Left Behind* books, and it is clear that the issue needs to be addressed. Almost all belief systems relating to the certainty of the Second Coming are linked to the uniquely odd New Testament book of Revelation. Revelation belongs to the historical writing style of "apocalyptic" literature, known for its imagery and symbolism. In essence, it was a secretive style of writing, a form of code text that was designed for the initiated only. This type of literature flourished between 200 BC and AD 100, which would have included the pre-Christ Hebrews and the full formative years of the church.

Unfortunately, two realities exist that make Revelation unreliable in establishing with exactness the timing of Christ's return: first, it was never intended to do so, which is a fact that has gone in and out of vogue over the history of the church; and second, it was written in code and the key has been lost since the second century. Unfortunately, neither of these facts has stopped some in the church from using and abusing the book of Revelation over time. In the early centuries, few took Revelation as anything more than a historical work addressed to the late first-century church that was under intense persecution from Rome and militant Jews. Centuries later, Revelation 20 became a jumping-off point for a specific theology that viewed the return of Jesus as a future event that would include the rapture of believers, a period of tribulation, and a final battle of Armageddon. The mega-popular *Left Behind* series is based on this theological view known as premillennial dispensationalism. What all of this means is that Paul saw his readers as living in the "later times," and, ironically, so does much of the modern church. In short, Jesus did not return for the early church, nor has he made it back by the time of this writing. So this portion of Paul's letter is directly applicable to the modern reader and, in effect, transcends the centuries of the church.

Demons in the Midst

Paul warns Timothy that in the later times people will turn away from the truth and accept the teachings of anti-Christian leaders. While Ephesus and the bulk of the Greco-Roman world was quite pagan, Paul was not concerned with the culture as much as with the fate of the church. He wrote Timothy about teaching within the church that could be deemed demonic. The Greek word translated "demon" (*daimonian*) was common and familiar, and Ephesian Christians would not necessarily have considered it evil. Socrates claimed to be guided by personal *daimonia*, and such spirits dominated most Greek religions. Paul was relating common beliefs with the evil that can accompany any and all contrary teachings, thus his reference to "deceitful spirits" (1 Tim 4:1). Paul was not the first to teach against demonic influence on the church.

> . . . In the last time there will be scoffers who will follow their own ungodly desires. These are the men who divide you, who follow mere natural instincts and do not have the Spirit (Jude 17-19).

> Jesus said to them: "Watch out that no one deceives you. Many will come in my name, claiming, 'I am he,' and will deceive many" (Mark 13:5).

> For false Christs and false prophets will appear and perform signs and miracles to deceive the elect—if that were possible (Mark 13:22).

Deceitful spirits and demonic influence did indeed wreak havoc with the elect, those who professed faith in Christ, and was a demonstrable problem for several hundred years of church history. The New Testament consistently presents God's provision of the Holy Spirit as protection against the unspiritual influences of demonically inspired teaching, but for many reasons the early church did not seek such assistance. The influence of false teachers grew within the church despite the wise counsel from Jesus, Paul, and Mark. Oddly, much of today's *Left Behind* theology focuses on a specific "Antichrist," even though the term does not appear in Revelation in any form. This term only appears in the John letters:

> Dear children, this is the last hour; and as you have heard that the antichrist is coming, even now many antichrists have come. Who is the liar? It is the man who denies that Jesus is the Christ. Such a man is the antichrist—he denies the Father and the Son (1 John 2:18, 22).

> Many deceivers, who do not acknowledge Jesus Christ as coming in the flesh, have gone out into the world. Any such person is the deceiver and the antichrist (2 John 7).

Any and all antichrists were nothing more than unbelieving false teachers who professed a "different gospel." Paul had little tolerance for these competing views and zero tolerance for anyone who would cause division and alter progress within the church. In 1 Timothy 4:2, he calls them "hypocritical liars," a term reserved for those who are so separated from a Spirit-inspired truth that their "consciences have been seared by a hot iron." Thomas Oden states, "They pretend to be confessing Christ while they bow to idols. So blatant are their hypocrisies that it seems as if their conscience had become dead and hardened" (58). Actually, a surface reading here lets these false teachers off easily. H. H. Harvey is much tougher on them: "The thought is not that their conscience has become insensible, but that they stand self-convicted, consciously bearing the brand-marks of wrong doing. Thus these men, while professing to be guides to righteousness, had their own conscience covered with the brand-marks of sin" (49-50).

In fact, in 2 Timothy 3:1-5 Paul cites specific sins that will proliferate in the world in the last days. It should again be noted that Paul was referring to his time as the last days and not to a distant future event. As easy as it would be to add a future view to Pauline theology, it would nevertheless be incorrect to do so. He stated that from his time forward, people would be self-absorbed, arrogant, full of disrespect, out of control, hedonistic, and controlled by money. In the following verse (6) he indicates that these evil people are also part of the false teacher problems plaguing the church.

All false teachers and antichrists mentioned here and elsewhere were known for their twisting of Scripture and fascination with "endless genealogies and fables." Paul cites particular teaching in

1 Timothy 4:3: "They forbid people to marry and order them to abstain from certain foods." Many false sects of Christianity forbade certain foods and marital relations due to the belief that the body was inherently flawed with only the spirit being pure. In order to keep the spirit pure, one had to abstain from anything pleasurable, specifically certain foods and sexual relations within the sanctity of marriage. These patently non-New Testament views tore at the foundation of God's provisions and plans for people. Scripturally, the natural world is not seen as being evil in and of itself. It is the pervasive and natural sin condition that ushered in evil in the first place. Paul states, "For everything God created is good, and nothing is to be rejected if it is received with thanksgiving, because it is consecrated by the word of God and prayer" (1 Tim 4:4).

So anything God created is good and proper for the believer to enjoy? Even (fill in the blank)? Yes, *even* that, if one reads Paul's words correctly. Paul had to counter the stifling rules of the false teachers who restricted things arbitrarily. In doing so, he opened the doors to basically all things if, and this is a big *if*, we regard them with respect. One could take God's creation of sex to the point of sin by contemplating relationships outside of marriage. Would sex suddenly be bad? No; the choice would be wrong, but not God's creation. The same line of thought can be applied to food and drink, and the argument holds indefinitely. The false teachers proposed that they knew more than God about God's own creation. Paul rejected this reasoning and everything else these teachers stood for, effectively drawing a line in the sand in regard to orthodox theology. The differences were stark and are summed up well in the Life Application Commentary: "Given the declaration by hypocritical liars that marriage and food are bad, alongside God's affirmation that these are beneficial, who are you going to believe?" (80).

Timothy's Training Regime

Imagine Paul looking over the varied landscape of the struggling Ephesus church and being unsettled about the future. He must have wondered if Timothy had what it would take to battle successfully the sinister forces of Greek pagan influence and false teaching. Even Paul's tireless cheerleading and support might not be enough to turn the tide. It was up to Timothy to rescue the church from the false teachers and restore the pure gospel to the people and city of Ephesus. A stickler might suggest that it was not up to Timothy at all since God holds the power against evil. That view would be more "pie-in-sky" than genuinely true, as God effectively left Paul and Timothy in charge. It is convenient and secure to place God on a white horse riding to the rescue with a host of angels, but in reality, Timothy would be the one standing up to false teaching and bad theology in Ephesus. However, God would empower Timothy as a redeemed, Spirit-filled believer who could stand against all things opposing Christ.

The stakes were high, so Paul reminded Timothy to do certain things in preparation for the battles he would face in Ephesus. In 1 Timothy 4:6, Paul writes, "If you point these things out to the brothers, you will be a good minister of Christ Jesus, brought up in the truths of the faith and of the good teaching that you have followed." In 2 Timothy 2:2, Paul writes, "And the things you have heard me say in the presence of many witnesses entrust to reliable men who will also be qualified to teach others." Paul is commanding Timothy to transfer to others the teaching he has received so more and more believers will be primed to stand against false teaching. If false teachers were the early church's worst enemy, the battles would be won through edification and education. Timothy would be more builder than soldier, working to create a solid foundation of Christians who were grounded in the truths of the faith. First, however, Timothy himself would have to continue to learn and train toward a new level of godliness. Paul obviously realized that Timothy would not be able to take the people farther than he himself had grown. In 2 Timothy 1:6-7, he tells Timothy, "I remind you to fan into flame the gift of God, which is in you through the laying on of hands. For God did not give us a spirit of timidity, but a spirit of power, of love and of self-discipline." This self-discipline is necessary for optimum growth in the Christian faith. Timothy would be able to call upon this power as he battled the forces of evil within the church. Timothy would need to demonstrate this type of love in order to lead people past the corrupt teaching and into the security of genuine faith knowledge.

In verse 7, Paul instructs Timothy to "have nothing to do with godless myths and old wives' tales; rather, train yourself to be godly." Timothy must resist the path of least resistance and fully reject the prevailing line of thought and teaching. Unfortunately, poor theology often makes natural sense and is easier to accept than the gospel. Jesus basically raised the bar on personal morality and conduct, and in the process he made faith living more difficult and demanding. This would also be true when contrasting the new faith against Judaism.

Imagine a Hebrew listening to the words of Jesus on adultery: "You have heard that it was said, 'Do not commit adultery.' But I tell you that anyone who looks at a woman lustfully has already committed adultery with her in his heart" (Matt 5:27-28). "Hmmm," the Hebrew might muse, "I think I'll stick with the Law!" Timothy's full-time focus would have to be on growing in faith maturity with little time spent on the opposing philosophies and lines of thought. John Calvin wrote, "It is as if Paul is saying, 'There is no reason why you should tire yourself with any other matters, which are all pointless. You will do the most valuable thing if you devote yourself only to godliness, using all your zeal and ability'" (73).

This is a bold contrast by Paul considering the wealth of prestige and history provided to bodily athletics. The forerunner of the modern Olympics was born in the Greco-Roman world Timothy served. To be an athlete was to be a hero and a privileged person. To train full-time for athletic pursuits was seen as the zenith of self-discipline. By applying the same Greek word used for athletic training (*gymnasia*) to faith development, Paul elevated spiritual exercise to the same lofty levels as Olympic-like pursuits. Timothy was to train with all his focus and might to be a "good minister" (1 Tim 4:6). Personal spiritual growth happens neither by osmosis nor accident; rather, it occurs through attending to study, prayer, and practice. One has to train in order to run five miles, and, conversely, one has to train to "know" correct Scripture and theology. When Paul stated that "physical training is of some value, but godliness has value for all things" (1 Tim 4:8), he was not dismissing physical exercise. Instead, he was elevating the need for spiritual training. Nothing, he inferred, is more important than working toward spiritual growth, maturity, and excellence. Paul sums this up in his letter to the Corinthian church: "Everyone who competes in the games goes into strict training. They do it to get a crown that will not last; but we do it to get a crown that will last forever" (1 Cor 9:25).

Paul also instructed young Timothy not to allow his age to become a hindrance to his overarching ministry. Obviously Paul was ordaining the "new guard" to lead what would soon become the next generation of the church. Unlike our culture in which youth is absurdly worshiped, the Greco-Roman world valued age and experience. H. H. Harvey calculates Timothy's age at the time of Paul's letters as approximately thirty-five years (54). If this is reliable, Timothy would not have had the immediate respect that came with years of life, and he would have been required to earn his platform. So that no one would "look down on his youth," Paul told Timothy to be exemplary in "speech, in life, in love, in faith, and in purity" (1 Tim 4:12). Timothy's primary impact on the people would come through actively "living" the faith. As he spoke, lived, and loved people, he would overcome the cultural hindrance of his youth and be in a position to reach and lead people. This, accompanied by devotion to the public proclamation of teaching and preaching Scripture, would result in the primacy of the genuine gospel holding sway in the fragmented church.

Timothy was instructed to be both genuine and real in his faith and to allow the integrity of Christ to be displayed in all areas of life. This alone would signal a monumental departure from the various false and pernicious teachings in play at the Ephesian church. By living what he taught, Timothy would display the reality and power inherent in the gospel. That is a primary difference between false theology and the genuine gospel of Christ. False teachers and antichrists were effectively "going it alone," whereas Timothy would have the Spirit of God as a traveling partner.

Life Lessons

The early church bears little resemblance to the church of today in any form, including intent and focus. We could read this statement as an indictment that the church lost its way at some point in history. This reading would be unfair, however, as the realities are much more abstract than they appear. The early church was engulfed in a geo-political dynasty that literally created and defined the culture. It also faced opposition from the varied Greek religions and from hostile Judaism. Add into the mix the plague of unorthodox teachers and itinerant philosophers who infiltrated the church with negative ideas, and you begin to see the level of difficulties faced by the first Christians. In contrast, the modern church is the product of 2,000 years of sophisticated splits and schisms. One would be hard pressed to find the "church" today, as it has disintegrated into multiple expressions of the biblical original.

Even though the fragmented and incohesive movement of today is operating freely in America and continues to hold some level of societal sway, it does share a few issues with the earliest believers. The church must continually guard itself against the demonic onslaught that has always been present in the world. False and incomplete teaching also continues to be problematic for the church. To believe that the educated and inclusive modern church is beyond the reach of unorthodox teaching would be a mistake. Look no further than *The Da Vinci Code* and *The Gospel of Judas* to find ancient aberrant texts that continue to lead people astray. Oddly, we also share a focus on the end of time with earlier Christians, albeit one in a different form. While they saw Jesus returning and the new spiritual order immediately taking effect, many people today foresee the return accompanied by battles between beasts, dragons, and demons against angels. In the modern version, the drama occurs over a period of several years rather than in a matter of seconds as the early Christians believed. My, haven't we come a long way in 2,000 years?

To best honor Paul's words, we should focus on the historical issues the church will always face. Demonic influence and false teaching will remain until the day Christ returns. We must not allow these negative influences to take hold in any form. We are still under Christ's command to bring the gospel to the lost world, which, by the way, is much bigger than ever before. We must also continue to make personal spiritual growth and Christian maturity a primary goal of life. If we progress in these areas, we will make the same level of difference that Paul called for in the first century. Yes, we are different, but we are also much the same.

1. In what ways does demonic influence continue to damage one's faith?

_____

_____

_____

_____

_____

_____

2. Cite hallmarks of false teaching.

_____

_____

_____

_____

_____

3. Discuss the modern fascination with the end of time and how it impacts the church.

_____

_____

_____

_____

_____

_____

_____

4. Name ways that false teaching can be problematic in the modern church.

_____

_____

_____

_____

_____

_____

_____

5. If God's creation is essentially good, why do we abstain from certain things for spiritual reasons? Explain.

_____

_____

_____

_____

_____

_____

_____

Timothy's Laundry List
1 Timothy 5:1–6:16; Titus 2:1-14

Paul's practical instruction to Timothy takes on new direction and dimension in 1 Timothy 5. Thus far in these letters, Paul has tackled weighty personal and church problems relating to false teaching, church leadership, women's issues, and pointed instruction to Timothy as an individual minister. Now we see Paul moving to more general instruction for Timothy as the young man takes the leadership reins of the varied and dysfunctional Ephesus church. This "laundry list" is weighted with topics related to differing groups and stages of adulthood found in the particular church at Ephesus. Themes such as these are common to Paul's teaching, but, while most have universal value, it is important to remember that Paul was not writing to the church of today. Despite the modern views of scriptural inerrancy and instant and absolute applicability, Paul's writing counted the future in days rather than centuries. A case in point found in this chapter is the teaching on slaves. While Paul did not make a case for the institution of slavery, he did advocate the status quo opinion of other writers of Scripture. *If you find yourself a slave, be a good slave* seems to be the quick take on slavery in the New Testament. If Paul had the church of two millennia later in mind, hopefully he would not have thought slavery to be a continuing human rights issue. Surely the church would have led in the eradication of such an inhumane and inequitable social malady over the centuries.

In fact, a case could be made that Paul was advocating an evolving change within each individual believer that over time would, or at least could, lead to massive social changes. If this is as true as I believe it to be, then the missives should be directed not at Paul, but at the church that has had 2,000 years to season the world with "salt and light." Paul's plan resembles pure genius when viewed from the reverse lens of time. With precious days, months, and possibly years in which to change the world, Paul sought a fundamental change in the lives of the new believers. This is evident in how he instructed Timothy to confront the false teachers within the church. Rather than excommunication or force, Paul opted for quiet dialogue and love. It was a counterculture approach then, and, sadly, it would be much the same today. The foundation of the change effect would be interpersonal and based on both integrity and consistent righteousness. In order to effect this type of massive change, we would need to separate "religion" from genuine "faith." In Paul's time, the worship of Caesar was a "religion," but it would be difficult to argue that it was remotely "faith." To Paul, faith would result in alteration, change, and difference, with each of the three being equally represented in both the individual Christian and society.

> For Paul, "the gospel" creates the church; "justification" defines it. The gospel announcement carries its own power to save people and to dethrone the idols to which they had been bound. "The gospel" itself is neither a system of thought, nor a set of techniques for making people Christians; it is the personal announcement of the person of Jesus. That is why it creates the church; the people who believe that Jesus is Lord and that God raised him from the dead. "Justification" is then the doctrine which declares that whoever believes that gospel, and wherever and whenever they believe it, those people are truly members of his family, no matter where they came from, what colour their skin may be, whatever else might distinguish them from each other. The gospel itself creates the church; justification continually reminds the church that it is the people created by the gospel and the gospel alone, and that it must live on that basis. (Wright, 151)

Tom Wright, British pastor and writer, goes on to add the element of "participationist" theology to Paul's writing. Participationist theology means "belonging to the people of God as redefined around the Messiah" (152). In simple, non-theological terminology, this means the people of God belong to each other and to the world of peoples "out there" in need of a "faith" based not on religion but on the Messiah Christ. The ancient Hebrews saw all aspects of faith as primarily corporate, from the way God interacted with them to how they dealt with other people groups. Jesus severely altered that view and practice with an intensely personal relationship centered in each believer. The next level of faith living would require each Christian to replicate that type of relationship with other people. If seen through the full scope of grace, no people type or group would ultimately be disenfranchised from grace, salvation, or justification. Thus human-on-human offenses such as slavery, racism, and oppression would gradually fade among those who claim faith in Christ. There is no doubt that over time, many cultures have greatly reduced such social negatives. This is especially true of our own society, but the question remains: Did the church play the largest role in the progression of equality?

Another reality that differentiates the early church from its modern counterpart in the West is the disparity among its adherents. The early church was built upon the lower classes and predominated by the classic "have nots" of society. This isn't to say the church was devoid of educated and wealthy people—it wasn't—but it illustrates that many early believers were themselves victims of discrimination and oppression due to their social status. Wayne Meeks cites second-century pagan writer Celsus on the makeup of the early church:

> Celsus, the first pagan author we know of who took Christianity seriously enough to write a book against it, alleged that the church deliberately excluded educated people because the religion was attractive only to "the foolish, dishonorable and stupid, and only slaves, women, and little children." He lived in the second century but he was sure that Christianity had always been a movement of the lowest classes, for Jesus himself had only been able to win disciples among "tax collectors and sailors, people who had not even a primary education." (51)

Obviously Celsus was biased against the new faith and did a great deal of "ax grinding" in his exposé of the church; but he did accurately point out that the earliest adherents of Jesus were from the lower socioeconomic groups. This fact makes Paul's instructions on equality and respect for women, the poor, widows, and the elderly even more amazing. Paul was advocating a revolution of sorts within the existing social order that would effectively change the way humans treat each other. This *agape*-love-based change would lead people to Christ in relational ways rather than scaring them with eternal damnation and sulphuric inhalation, which is a caricature of the twentieth century's approach to evangelism. This seems once again to prove that the modern church has not yet assimilated Paul's message.

Older and Younger

Jesus was indeed a social reformer who literally rescripted the patterns of response and attention to the many and various needs of his day. Paul followed in his steps and, in effect, brought Jesus' teaching to the next generation. It must be pointed out that neither of them bowed to the norm of instilling political or economic motivations into their social messages. For both Jesus and Paul, the impetus of social care through the church was based entirely on morality. According to Walter Rauschenbusch, "Jesus had realized the life of God in the soul of man and the life of man in the love of God as being the real secret of his life, and as the wellspring of his purity, his compassion, his unwearied courage, and his unquenchable idealism" (48). Possibly, it is the idealism of Jesus to which Paul held most in his theology of ministry. To say "why not" rather than "that's the way it is" is the difference between most cultures and the idealism of Jesus and Paul. Such idealism seems to drive Paul in his instructions to Timothy regarding stages of life within the church and culture.

It is positive to note at this point that Paul did have in mind universal relationships as he taught Timothy. The early church bears absolutely no resemblance to the modern church, save the primary focus of Jesus. The early believers practically lived together, sharing a fully common life built around a completely common faith. They prayed together, ate together, and studied together, most commonly in homes. In some cities, worship continued to take place in the temple, but all other activities centered in the homes. If the first church were this close and intimate, then Paul's instructions would have been tantamount to "preaching to the choir." Proper relationships would be easiest to undertake and maintain within the Christian community, even amongst the problematic teachers. If, however, Paul's words were applied in the overall context of life and "lived" out among all people, then a genuine Christian difference could be evidenced. Thus, Paul's instructions should be taken in the broadest sense possible.

Paul's first focus is how to treat older men. It has already been established that Timothy was young, approximately mid-thirties, and that his age could have easily become a liability in the culture of the day. Age was revered and respected as a general rule in the

Greco-Roman world, with exceptions being made for the poorest or sickest. If Timothy was to speak with authority, especially to older men propagating false doctrines, he must learn to do so in a way that would best lead to acceptance. Paul suggests treating all older men with the same respect provided to a father. This might seem like an overly simplistic thought, but it may have been important knowledge for Timothy, who was brought up mainly by his mother and grandmother.

Paul's instruction "Do not rebuke an older man harshly, but exhort him as if he were your father" (1 Tim 5:1) contains two words that do not edify in the least. Literally, "rebuke" and "harshly" signify verbal tension that is more pedagogy than adult correction. It is one thing to speak down to a child (possibly not always the best thing), but quite another to do so to an older adult. Leviticus 19:32 demonstrates a proper practice of the Hebrews: "Rise in the presence of the aged, show respect for the elderly."

It is important to see the long view of Paul's commands to Timothy and Titus regarding the handling of older men. Both Timothy and Titus were young but were nonetheless in positions requiring them to correct older people. Success would require relationships based on respect that allowed for corrective, orthodox teaching. Titus 2:1 reads, "You must teach what is in accord with sound doctrine." In Crete and Ephesus, sound doctrine was neither popular nor consistently well received. Despite that certainty, both men were required to teach the truth out of respect, honor, and love.

This same line of thought is taught for the treatment of older women. Since women were restricted from upper leadership and teaching roles in the Ephesus church, this instruction would suggest treatment of women in general. Women were to be respected in much the same manner and practice as a mother would be by a son. "Older women as mothers" (v. 2) places the older female at a prized level that would literally demand respect and honor. This would not be the natural case for younger women, however, as the culture of the day did not show abundant respect for women. With the virtual caste system in place for women in Ephesian society and the negative sexual roles filled by younger women in the various pagan religions, younger women did not necessarily fare well. Of course, Paul was advocating a counterculture reaction toward people in general, and women specifically, within the new order of the Christian church.

This new mindset is never more evident than in his teaching toward younger women: "Younger women as sisters, with absolute purity" (v. 2). The term "purity" is important for understanding the level of respect Paul is commanding toward younger women. In an age and culture as rife with sexual exploitation as first-century Ephesus, Paul instructed that younger women should be treated as one would treat family, specifically a sister. Thus, the very thought of sexual interaction had to be disallowed if women were to be treated with the purest of intentions. Paul used much the same language in telling Timothy to live with purity in order to be the proper example (1 Tim 4:12). There would be simply no room for ulterior motives of any sexual nature when dealing with younger women. Once again, the new faith would be completely counterculture.

Paul takes a different tack with younger women in the Titus letter. In respect to the Crete church, proper treatment of younger women combined with the counsel of older women would allow for better wives and mothers. Reverent older women would model and encourage younger women to be pure, loving, and honoring of God. This symbiotic structure would be wholly dependent on the overall environment of proper and equal treatment provided women in general.

Widows

"Honor widows who are really widows" (v. 3) seems to be more riddle than sensible statement to the modern reader. Obviously, there was some level of chicanery present in Ephesus by select widows who sought support. To care for the needs of widows was a longstanding practice of the Hebrews and one quickly adopted by the followers of Christ. James wrote one of the most Hebrew-like New Testament books and in it advocates, "Religion (faith) that God our Father accepts as pure and faultless is this: look after orphans and widows in their distress" (1:27). To care for those with no social safety net was a prime ministry of the early church, and obviously it was not one taken lightly. Due to the fact that resources were undoubtedly limited among the believers, special scrutiny was given to ensure care was provided for the neediest of people. Walter Liefeld sets forth implications based on these verses: "The text implies that the following questions were being asked in the church: (1) Which widows truly are in need? (2) What is the responsibility of family and other relatives? (3) How can the church determine which widows qualify for inclusion on their list? (4) How should the church deal with women who do not qualify for the list?" (175)

The aforementioned Acts 6:1 cites the needs of widows as the primary reason the first men were chosen to serve within the church. As the church expanded and reached more people, the needs became exponentially more difficult to manage. As a result, the office of deacon became more and more systemized and, subsequently, so did the oversight of those in need. To manage this issue properly, Paul laid down specific guidelines for them to follow (vv. 3-12). First, the widow must be of genuine need, thus she would have no relatives who could provide support and care. Second, she must be at least sixty years of age. Third, she must have been faithfully married in the proper sense. Lastly, Paul cites the need for a good reputation in matters of faith, family, and service. Ironically, this teaching cements Paul's personal reputation for creating requirements for virtually all stations of life. Just as an overseer and deacon had specified requirements, so did the husbandless widow. It is probable that Paul couldn't shake off all of his former Hebrew habits.

These verses come together to answer Paul's earlier riddle as to who is a genuine widow (v. 3). A "widow who is really a widow" was one who met all the above qualifications. If Paul was trying to extend grace to those mired in widowhood, he missed, but if he was trying to reduce the overall number of women who would receive assistance, then he succeeded. One must question how many widows "made the cut," considering how strict the qualifiers seem to be. Plus, nothing is mentioned about recent converts who previously may not have led exemplary lives. Would they be "grandfathered" (or better yet, "grandmothered") in? Paul isn't clear on this point, so one must assume that the rules were strictly adhered to in most early locales.

One other point that suggests additional severity in the oversight of widows focused on younger widows under sixty years of age. Paul deemed such widows as not eligible for church support. In reality, younger widows had more options than older widows, with remarriage being the most obvious and accessible. In fact, Paul tells them to find another mate, have children, and manage the household rather than seek assistance from the church (v. 15). Of course, Paul cites the noblest of all options only after he states the possibilities of their becoming gossipers, slanderers, and busybodies if the church takes care of them. While this might not have been the most positive of all implications, he no doubt had real reasons for this worry aside from the known women who had already succumbed to false teaching.

Ministers

Paul's next laundry list topic concerns church leaders, specifically those who preach and teach. Paul's view is that the preachers and teachers who lead the church are due "double honor" (v. 17). The term used here is unique both to Paul and this verse and thus has an ambiguous meaning. Scholars differ as to whether Paul referred to respect, to remuneration, or to a combination of both. It is obvious from the preceding verses detailing proper respect for older men and women that honor accorded to age was the cultural ideal. However, it seems that Paul was once again infusing his own performance standards into the mix. In order to gain this double honor, a leader must perform his or her job "well." Possibly the best method of understanding this verse is to view it through the lens of the false teaching problem. Paul was undoubtedly separating those who were orthodox and genuine from those who espoused erroneous theology and had impure motives. But what about paying the minister? Again, Paul seems to be inferring a professional-level ministry station that was to receive a heavy amount of respect and proper remuneration.

Paul's Old and New Testament references to "do not muzzle the ox" (Deut 25:4) and "the worker deserves his wages" (Luke 10:7) support financial compensation for ministers. This concept is neither unique nor new, as 2 Chronicles stipulates paying the priests in order for them to "devote themselves to the law of the Lord" (31:4). Paul also uses much the same language in 1 Corinthians 9 to make the case for clergy support, and in total he seems to be reinforcing the Old Testament view that complete devotion to ministry requires the church to cover basic life expenses. If Timothy were to solve the multitude of issues facing the Ephesus church and lead them to grow and reach people, he would need to devote all his time and effort to the task. If he were forced to take on a side job in order to "pay the bills," ministry would suffer. Once again, Paul was thinking of the greater kingdom needs and not getting bogged down in the temporal minutiae that so often captures the church.

Slaves

Paul's continued teaching on slavery is possibly the most difficult for modern readers to reconcile (1 Cor 7:20-24; Eph 6:5-9; Col 3:22-25; Titus 2:9-10; Philemon). Despite the fact that slavery has been part of the human predicament throughout all of recorded history, including today's world, most people too easily shuffle it off to anti-quation. It would be an equal mix of fallacy and wishful thinking to see slavery as nothing more than an ancient problem. It exists today, and chances are it will continue to exist well into the future. As long as there are evil people who amass control of vast resources and power, human-on-human abuses will result. So, if slavery is an unspeakable evil and obviously at odds with the words of Jesus in Galatians 3:28, why did Paul not take an abolishment stance? Why did he and Peter allow for the status quo and, worse, command slaves to honor their owners? Sadly, the answers won't mesh well with modern approaches to dealing with human abuses. The Greco-Roman world utilized slavery to an extent that was on par with ancient Egypt. To say that it was pervasive would be understate-ment, as it is estimated that sixty million slaves served at the time of Paul's letter. To frame it differently, there were as many slaves as there were free people during that era. To command a sudden end to an institutionalized practice of that magnitude would have led to revolt, anarchy, and the might and power of Rome falling upon the new church.

Rather than command slaves to leave their situation and cause massive social upheaval, it seems Paul opted for the slower, more spiritual route. He created guidelines for slaves to follow in relating to their owners based on respect: "All who are under the yoke of slavery should consider their masters worthy of full respect, so that God's name and our teaching may not be slandered" (1 Tim 6:1). As mentioned earlier in this session, despite Paul's not having a true long-term view of the church, he nonetheless proposed living in a manner that would evoke a slow change in all social areas. The notion of being seasoning agents for the entire world was at the heart of Paul's instructions for his church and, consequently, the one that followed.

Root of All Evil

Paul next ordered the "combination platter" of false teaching and motive onto the table of instruction. He took possibly his strongest shot at those who disagreed with sound theology and godly teaching, labeling them "conceited and understanding nothing" (vv. 3-4). These conceited false teachers were known by their "unhealthy interest in controversies and quarrels about words that result in envy, strife, malicious talk, evil suspicions and constant friction between men of corrupt mind, who have been robbed of the truth and who think godliness is a means to financial gain" (vv. 4-5). In these verses, Paul presents the spiritual and theological divide existing between the Christian and financial gain. A couple of questions are raised due to this section: Is the Christian to focus on financial wealth or spiritual progress? Is it possible to have both and allow wealth to remain subordinate to materialism?

The answer to the latter question is yes, one can be both spiritual and wealthy, but spiritual growth would need to remain the primary focus. The false teachers were apparently double scoundrels who propagated false gospels and *fleeced the flock* for financial gain. Paul speaks of certain women who were easy marks for the false teachers, but it seems obvious that their evil was equally spread. The lessons to be learned relate to the need for control of money in the lives of believers. It is clear that Paul never intended for money alone to be seen as evil, as money is inanimate. Rather, the love and desire for money is problematic for people of faith. Spiritual contentment (v. 6), never the temporal reality of money, should be the ultimate life goal for the Christian. Paul was stating to Timothy that spirituality transcends money and material goods. This reality was important for Timothy both to teach and model as he matured in his faith and leadership ministry. Plus, this truth is still greatly applicable to the modern believer and church.

Life Lessons

There is no controversy over the level of difficulty facing both Timothy and Titus as they assumed the positions Paul assigned. Each minister was young, inexperienced, and inherited troubled congregations. Nonetheless, Paul seemed to have unwavering faith in the spiritual depth and abilities of each man. In fact, these letters provided practical theology and administrative assistance to them in a way that suggests Paul held no doubt about their eventual successes. Even though Paul did not write these letters to the modern church, they contain a wealth of valuable insight and instruction that could improve the ministry impact of the church on the world. Imagine a world in which injustice against humankind is lessened or alleviated due to the influence of the church. Imagine a world permeated by grace rather than greed, brought about by the practiced faith of Christians. This "imagined" world does not yet exist, and some of the blame for the current state of the world rests squarely on the church. Putting genuine faith into practice is exactly what Paul asked Timothy to do. If Timothy modeled right behavior for the believers in Ephesus, Ephesus would change over time. This same possibility exists in our world as well. Wherever we live, we can make a positive impact through modeling and exhibiting Christian character. The century is irrelevant to this point, for whenever God's people produce righteousness, the world is changed to some degree.

The entire "laundry list" provided for Timothy could be applied to the modern life with only minimal contextualization. People continue to deserve respectful treatment: older women and men deserve a level of respect reserved for the experienced; younger men need role models and wise counsel; younger women deserve to be treated with propriety worthy of a sister; and money must never become a god. These instructions can make all lives better when understood and applied to daily faith living. Plus, larger social and cultural issues need influencing as well. It seems both confusing and sad that modern believers will rally for the display of the Ten Commandments yet remain silent on the poor, the enslaved, and those being slaughtered in the name of God. There is something spiritually wrong with the church when it fights for the easy and safe while ignoring the difficult and uncomfortable. Paul instructed Timothy and Titus always to take the more difficult path of ministry based on love and respect. In doing so, Paul created the biblical model for both ministry and spiritual existence. It's as if faith suddenly becomes a verb rather than a noun in the grammatical lexicon of Paul.

1. Paul utilizes metaphors when teaching about the church. How does his characterization of the church as "family" impact his instructions to Timothy and Titus?

_____

_____

_____

_____

_____

_____

2. Cite ways a younger leader can lead, teach, or correct an older person without being disrespectful.

_____

_____

_____

_____

_____

_____

3. Discuss reasons why today's society no longer seems to honor age and experience.

_____

_____

_____

_____

_____

_____

4. List ways older women could provide wise counsel to younger women within the church.

_____

_____

_____

_____

_____

_____

5. Discuss ways in which our culture has made it difficult for younger women to be treated with the chaste purity described by Paul.

_____

_____

_____

_____

_____

_____

6. Why do you think Paul differentiated widows in general from "those who are really widows"?

_____

_____

_____

_____

_____

_____

7. What should the modern church be doing to alleviate slavery and human rights abuses present in the world?

_____

_____

_____

_____

_____

_____

8. Discuss ways in which the love of money is the root cause of great evil.

_____

_____

_____

_____

_____

_____

9. Cite ways one could train and exercise for spiritual growth.

_____

_____

_____

_____

_____

_____

10. Are there still "myths, endless genealogies, and old wives' tales" that affect the church? Describe examples.

_____

_____

_____

_____

_____

_____

11. What is your personal view of God's timetable for the world, and how does it shape your faith practices?

_____

_____

_____

_____

_____

_____

12. What would be today's equivalent of "widows and orphans"?

_____

_____

_____

_____

_____

_____

Don't Be a Cretan

Titus 1; 2:1-8

Paul assigned his faithful assistant Titus to one of the most demand-ing leadership roles in the first-century church. Titus accompanied Paul on many missionary trips and became valuable as an adminis-trator and mediator. These gifts became evident in his extended relationships with the Corinthian church after they rebelled at Paul's leadership. Simultaneous with Timothy being sent to Ephesus, Titus was assigned the duty of establishing churches on the Greek island of Crete. Crete was not the normal Greek domain as Romans, Greek nationals, varieties of Hebrews, and an interchangeable population of seafarers populated it. Because it was a well-placed island, sea trade and ship traffic were major components of life on Crete. Other than the mountainous areas that reached 8,000 feet in height, the island was small and compact and allowed for efficient travel throughout the land. Crete was well known for its citizens' propensities for hard drinking, fighting, lying, and stealing. To be deemed a "Cretan" was anything but a compliment in the first century. The island was also famous for its preoccupation with the Greek deity Zeus and his fam-ily. Crete boasted that Zeus was a resident of the island, even opting for a human-type burial there. Possibly, this is one of the reasons Cretans weren't known for an abundance of truth and accuracy.

The Assignment

Paul states, "The reason I left you in Crete was that you might straighten out what was left unfinished and appoint elders in every town, as I directed you" (1:5). It is anyone's guess what Paul meant by "unfinished" things, but the other facet of responsibility is quite clear: Crete was ready to have multiple church locations, and Titus needed to select and train elders to establish and lead them. This may sound easy at first read; simply find the right people to place in charge of each church location and your job is done! The reason it most likely was not easy links to the fact that the average Cretan was, well, a *Cretan.* Viewing this situation through the lens of today's church, it is hard to imagine the level of difficulty Titus faced. Crete was for that century what the combination of Bourbon Street in New Orleans and the Las Vegas Strip is to our own. The moral climate was weaker there than in other portions of the Greco-Roman world, and when combined with the large numbers of Greek pagan worshipers, it created a climate for self-indulgent behaviors and mindsets.

Nevertheless, Titus was asked to bring the light of the Christian message to the disorderly land of Crete. Just as in the Timothy letters, Paul focuses on the unique qualifications of those who will serve the churches. At first read, these qualifications seem to be exact duplicates of those Paul delineated for the Ephesian church (1 Tim 3:1-7). They are indeed similar, but Paul actually spends less time and space on qualifications in the Titus letter and more on the deficiencies of the people in general.

Perhaps this is because Titus was also privy to the Timothy letters or simply because the residents on Crete were especially immoral. Either way, Paul instructed Titus straightaway to find and appoint individuals who would lead the fellowships of believers. It seems important to note that unlike in Ephesus, Paul was moving the church on Crete from one corporate grouping to one in multiple locations. This is a departure from the average framework of the church at this point in history. It is, however, the exact structure that allowed for the church of the following century to grow and expand in scope and population. The Life Application Commentary succinctly defines the unique nature of the Crete leadership model: "(1) local, (2) multiple, (3) qualified" (255).

Qualifications

Just as in the Ephesian plan (1 Tim 3:1-7; 5:22), qualifications relate more to character than to intelligence or ability. The first qualification is *blameless* (1:6). Elders must show a history of being above reproach by having lived in such a manner that charges could not be successfully brought against them. Liefield defines this as having an "untarnished reputation" (312). Stott uses "unquestioned integrity, but not flawless or faultless, or we would all be disqualified" (175). The idea of complete integrity fits well in this qualification, as it would be an outstanding personal virtue and quality in that particular environment. The next qualifier is *the husband of but one wife* (1:6). While this is almost identical to the Timothy letter's qualification for overseer, the addition of *but* changes the entire discussion. For the past 100 years, the pattern has been to take such verses as literally as possible in order to sustain an all-male clergy (Baptist practice). To that end, the third chapter of 1 Timothy is utilized much more often to diagram qualifiers than this section of Titus. It is amazing that one word could be at the heart of this preference for Timothy's letter. Despite this reality, it is imperative to view all "like" sections of Scripture before establishing theology and practice. Only when Scripture is properly attended to can it become the guide and path to truth and order.

To be the husband of *but* one wife focused on the primacy of the spousal relationship and the exclusion of any activities that would interfere with a closed relationship. World-renowned British pastor and writer John Stott sums it up this way:

> The conclusion reached is that it is not intended to exclude from the pastorate either those who have never married or remarried widowers, but rather the polygamous and those who have remarried after divorce. More generally and positively, ministerial candidates must have an unsullied reputation in the whole area of sex and marriage. (175)

While these renderings clear up issues related to gender, they do not seem to allow for leaders who have divorced and later remarried. Please note that none of this seems to be predicated on divorce, but on the marriage following divorce. S. M. Baugh of Westminster Seminary cites the prevalence of divorce in the Greco-Roman culture of the first century and explains that either party, including the wife's father, could obtain divorce for nearly any reason. Barren women could be divorced due to childlessness, and Greek men could divorce in order to "trade up" for wealthier women within their own clan. Baugh suggests Paul was referring primarily to the practice by both Greeks and Romans of concubinage, which included young girls and boys (501). Crete was historically known for pederasty, the practice of older men taking in young boys for tutelage, refinement, and "other" services. It is obvious that any and all of these practices would be bad reflections on the church, which taught a firm moral code based on Christ's life and message. All things considered, marital fidelity is the best definition of Paul's marital qualification for elder.

The elder's family is also focused upon and includes believing children who are not seen as *wild and disobedient* (1:6). The family is a microcosm of the church and could be used to determine if the elder candidate is effective in leading, modeling, and affirming people in general. If one's children are believers and have been taught the truths of Scripture, he or she will likely be successful in teaching and leading the whole of the church. In contrast, how can a person lead and effect change in a body of believers if he or she hasn't first been effective at home? Paul next lists traits that a prospective elder must not embody: *not overbearing, not quick-tempered, not given to drunkenness, not violent, not pursuing dishonest gain* (1:7). "Overbearing" is a term often defined as "arrogant" (2 Pet 2:10), "self-willed," and "stubborn." None of these could be seen as positives for a church leader in any circumstance and thus must be avoided. Quick-tempered is an indicator of a bent toward explosive anger that goes beyond simply losing one's temper. This term carries an inherent likelihood of also losing self-control. Again, it is not a character trait befitting a church leader.

Drunkenness is most literally translated as not given to an overindulgence in wine. Wine was ordinary and prevalent in that society, and one would expect the same within the church. In fact, a pure prohibition against drinking alcohol is not found in the New Testament. This means that with the option of drinking wine also comes a responsibility to do so with great judgment. Responsible drinking in Paul's time held implications that would be foreign to today's church. That said, however, similarities also exist, and the greatest of these would be the realization that leadership is always accompanied by unique expectations. To abuse alcohol in the slightest way would be to undermine the integrity of the whole church.

The fact that violence is not to be practiced by the church leader would seem to be a given, but this actually was a problem for the early church. Chroniclers tell us that it was not uncommon for bishops and elders to punish wayward believers physically or to come to blows with those who disagreed with their views or practices. Several Apostolic Canons include phrases such as "It is ordered that a bishop who strikes an erring believer should be deposed" (Barclay, 271). Considering the words and vivid actions of Jesus, this injunction against pugilistic elders should be easy to honor. To resist dishonest gain would be a positive character trait for the elder as the opportunity for cheating and manipulating the system would be ever-present.

Paul shifts from the "do nots" to the "dos" as he completes the qualification profile for elders on Crete: "Rather he must be hospitable, one who loves what is good, who is self-controlled, upright, holy and disciplined" (1:8). Hospitality is taking heed of the welfare of others and has a literal meaning of "lover of strangers." The opportunity to meet and tend to travelers would be common on a transient, commercial island like Crete. To love what is good is to be righteously minded in all things with a focus on the positive. Often the best way to distinguish these qualifications is to contrast them with their exact opposites. The flip side of good would be bad and the opposite of righteousness would be unrighteousness, so making this connection should be easy. Self-controlled is dealt with repeatedly in the Pastoral Epistles and holds the same meanings in each case. To be upright is to be honest and above reproach in all relationships. To be holy is to be different due to a unique devotion, in this case to Christ. The believer, specifically the leader, must have an agenda that is larger than himself or herself. According to Paul, a love for Jesus must dominate this agenda. "Disciplined" does not appear elsewhere in the New Testament but likely has to do with progressive spiritual exercise and practice that leads to maturity and holiness.

A disciplined believer and leader would be one who held firm to the essence of the gospel of Christ, proclaiming the message to those in need, and defending it against the already present opposition (v. 9). J. N. D. Kelly writes in *The Pastoral Epistles*, "The two-fold task of building up the faithful and eliminating error" is the "chief challenge" of the Crete leadership (32). It certainly stands to reason that a leader must be well grounded spiritually, but does this mean no diversity of opinion could exist? Is the church not built on some level of personal theology? With the amount of focus provided false theology, it would seem that proper theology is a one-way street of ideals. This isn't the case, of course, as there is a fully delineated line between the absolutes of Scripture and everything else that falls under the umbrella of free interpretation. Perhaps it is accurate to admit that this freedom has been overdone and abused over the centuries, but this freedom has allowed for the "absolutes" to hold such power. It is also important to point out that the original church was one in origin and practice, and it was not until much later that splits began to promote the interpretational issues over the absolutes. This would be another case of Paul being far ahead of his time as he formatted the church. By promoting the absolutes above all else, he was able to provide foundational adhesive and keep the church on a single track. This fact would be of utmost importance for the church on Crete as Titus would be battling negative forces from within while simultaneously trying to reach the uniquely odd people of Crete.

The Audience

Suffice it to say, Crete was not an average place, and Cretans were not average people. In fact, Cretans were widely known and vilified in the Greco-Roman world as liars, cheats, and brawlers. This suggests that Titus must have drawn the proverbial short straw in being assigned to expand the church on Crete. It may also suggest that no one other than Titus held the unique gifts and skills to accomplish such an outwardly difficult assignment. The unique difficulties facing Titus were similar to those Timothy confronted in Ephesus, namely intellectual and philosophical notions, Gnosticism, and radical Hebrew elements. Greeks were known for a quasi-spiritual/quasi-philosophical line of thinking that routinely diminished the deity of Jesus. Gnosticism claimed a special knowledge necessary to attain salvation. The full discussion on Gnosticism appears in session 1 above. In short, Gnostics believed multiple emanations of God were required to effect creation through natural and corrupted matter. To find salvation a person must learn to navigate the multitude of mini-gods in order to reach the God above it all. Suspiciously absent from their salvation equation are the acts of Jesus Christ. To this end, they were known for their use of long genealogies and fables.

The most obvious culprit of unorthodox teaching on Crete, however, was the "circumcision" group. The norm is to see this group as Judaizers, the early Hebrew converts who insisted on continuing Hebrew practices and requirements as Christians. According to James Blevins, Titus and Paul's opponents were Hebrew Christians who demanded adherence to Mosaic Law for Gentile converts to Christ. "Judaizers emphasized three major points: (1) salvation belonged to the children of Abraham; (2) gentiles could become adopted children of Abraham by accepting the initiatory rites of circumcision; and, (3) converts should keep the Jewish Law with particular emphasis on the food laws, feasts, and fasts" (632). This restrictive theology would fly in the face of Paul, who preached the full equality of Christ's sacrifice and subsequent salvation. Galatians 3:28 is regarded as the Magna Carta of the New Testament as it states the case for equality for all people groups in Christ: "There is neither Jew nor Greek, slave nor free, male nor female, for you are all one in Christ Jesus." Paul also utilized the Galatian letter to promote reliance on the Holy Spirit over the Jewish Law.

> All who rely on observing the law are under a curse, for it is written: "Cursed is everyone who does not continue to do everything written in the Book of the Law." Clearly no one is justified by God by the law, because, "The righteous live by faith." The law is not based on faith; on the contrary, "The man who does these things will live by them." Christ redeemed us from the curse of the law by becoming a curse for us, for it is written: "Cursed is everyone who is hung on a tree." He redeemed us in order that the blessing given to Abraham might come to the Gentiles through Christ Jesus, so that by faith we might receive the promise of the Spirit. (Gal 3:10-14)

Paul refers to this "circumcision" group in Titus 1:10 as "many rebellious people." A careful work-study provides the additional meaning of "insubordinate, or those who refuse to submit to the trustworthy message" (Stott, 180). Paul also depicts them as deceivers, meaning they actively led people astray. This would easily capture the intentional practices of a radical Hebrew group that worked toward a Christianized form of legalism. To this end, Paul used the analogy "To the pure all things are pure, but to those who are corrupted and do not believe nothing is pure; but even their minds and consciences are defiled" (1:15).

These false teachers were purity-deficient due to either a lack of spiritual maturity (legalism over Holy Spirit) or to the fact that they were not genuine believers in the first place. It appears their corruption was situated at core level, which suggests they were not essentially spiritual to begin with. Simply put, they were not what they purported themselves to be.

> . . . *they claim to know God,* boasting of their *gnosis, but by their actions they deny him* (1:16a). That is, there is a fundamental dichotomy between what they say and what they are, between their words and deeds. Usually professions and denials are opposites, which exclude one another. We cannot profess what we deny, or deny what we profess. At least, to do so is the essence of

hypocrisy, because then we profess God in word and deny him in deed. This is ritual without reality, form without power, claims without character, faith without works. (Stott, 183)

Liefeld adds,

It places responsibility on the apparently super-religious people, who carefully trace back the myths and rigorously seek purity by following their reconstruction of the ancient food laws. But in fact if they were truly pure, they would not be so obsessed with the need for such laws. Through their impure minds and consciences everything appears impure and so needs legalistic regulation. (317)

This is by and large a faith and works issue that had grown disproportionately large due to the immaturity of the Christians on Crete. To make matters worse, it appears all of the corrupted theology was being propagated by native Cretans. It had to be difficult for people who hailed from such a corrupted place readily to identify corrupted theology. They simply did not have a great deal to fall back upon spiritually.

The Job at Hand

The role for Titus is clearly laid out in 1:11: "Whose mouths must be stopped, who subvert whole households, teaching things which they ought not for the sake of dishonest gain." The false teachers disrupting the church on Crete must be stopped in order to preserve both the unity of the local church and the integrity of the gospel. The Greek word used here literally means "to muzzle." The false teachers were in the process of corrupting the faith lives of Cretan Christians. The church was losing ground as an agent of influence and seasoning for this secular and self-absorbed society. Titus needed to silence the false teachers of philosophy, Gnosticism, and Judaized Christianity if the church were to survive.

The Answer

The prescribed answer to the problems affecting the Crete church was a simple 180-degree turn from the methods utilized by the corrupted teachers. Titus was to counter their insidious effect with genuine theology matched by a righteous lifestyle. In these polar extremes, the truth of the gospel would break through. In the spiritual economy, truth always trumps untruth. It also stands to reason that over time untruths within the Christian community will lead to destruction. A careful word study underscores the absolute importance of Paul's use of "sound." The present participle of the verb form literally means "to be healthy." The sound teaching of Titus would not only negate the effects of bad theology and philosophy, but it would also lead to healthy believers. In Mark 5:34, John 5:9, and Acts 4:10, the adjective form is applied to Christian practice that is healthy in contrast to the sick or unhealthy teaching of false teachers.

So, with the prescription to "teach what is in accord with sound doctrine" (2:1) and "In everything set them an example" (2:7), Titus could "muzzle" and "silence" the false teachers on Crete. By combining a lifestyle and a message based on ultimate truth, the power of God can be displayed against the false, the corrupt, and the dying philosophies of humankind.

Life Lessons

Despite the fact that Paul omitted Titus from any mention in Acts, Titus was not a minor player in the development of the early church. The work Titus did for Paul in Corinth and later on Crete was instrumental in the progression of the church through difficult periods. Without the contributions of Titus, the church would not be what it is today. This proves that one person can make historic impact on the Christian movement. It should be a reality that is primary to the study of this letter; unfortunately, it is often lost in the overpowering focus on the lying, cheating, and brawling Cretans. It is difficult not to become consumed by the evil and decadence of the population of Crete. There must also be some level of vicarious wonder to it all as most modern believers have little frame of reference for such people. It is, however, in this environment that Titus stood firm for God and promoted the reality of the gospel.

Just as in the Timothy letters, we are provided with prescriptive qualifications for church leaders. Leaders must be above reproach and live overtly ethical lives. Leaders must practice marital purity in all forms. Leaders must first impact their own families for Christ before providing leadership to the church. Leaders must practice self-control in all areas of life, including temperament, money, alcohol, and relationships. Leaders must love people with a unique constancy. Above all else, leaders must be spiritually genuine and practice what they believe. These qualifications should remain in practice for the modern church just as they were for the first-century church. Plus, we should see them as necessary for each Christian and not reserved solely for leadership. To do otherwise would increase the already existent double standard of more being required of leaders than lay believers.

In many ways the dark and decadent world of first-century Crete is not so dissimilar to our own. People still live in a society that promotes lies and shortcuts in virtually all facets of life. Today's pluralistic religious and spiritual landscape does much to diminish the reality of Christ. The modern church is teetering on the brink of losing its capacity to influence the culture. One might think that over 2,000 years, the church would mature to the point of being the driving force in the world. This has not happened. The church is "on the outside looking in" in most regards, and one wonders if a comeback is even possible. Despite these dire circumstances, we must follow the words of Paul and seek to be salt and light to our world. The Crete church would not have made it to the second century if Titus had not lived and taught the truth. By "teaching what is in accord with sound doctrine" and "In everything set[ting] them an example," we can do our part to make a difference in our world. Titus did . . . so can we.

1. What were some of the unique problems Titus faced on Crete?

_____

_____

_____

_____

_____

_____

2. Cite ways a country that prided itself on Greek pagan worship might have a difficult time believing in Christ.

_____

_____

_____

_____

_____

_____

3. Epimendies, a teacher from the sixth-century BC, stated, "Cretans are always liars, evil brutes, lazy gluttons." How would these character traits make it difficult for Titus to evangelize there?

_____

_____

_____

_____

_____

4. Cite the qualifications Paul deemed necessary for leadership in the Crete church.

_____

_____

_____

_____

_____

5. How were the Gnostics impacting the Crete church?

_____

_____

_____

_____

_____

6. How were the Judaizers impacting the Crete church?

_____

_____

_____

_____

_____

7. Describe Paul's command for self-control as it relates to Titus's requirement always to set an example.

_____
_____
_____
_____
_____
_____

8. In short, describe the Christian message Titus was to teach through sound doctrine.

_____
_____
_____
_____
_____
_____

Bibliography

Bailey, Mark. *Nelson's New Testament Survey*. Nashville: Thomas Nelson, 1999.

Barclay, William. *The Letters to Timothy, Titus & Philemon*. Edinburgh Scotland: St. Andrew Press, 1960.

Baugh, Steven M. *1 & 2 Timothy & Titus*. Interpretation, A Bible Commentary. Canada: HarperCollins/Zondervan, 2002.

Blevins, James. In *Mercer Dictionary of the Bible*. Macon GA: Mercer University Press, 1997.

Calvin, John. *1 & 2 Timothy & Titus*. Wheaton IL/Nottingham England: Crossway Books, 1998.

Earle, Ralph. *Word Meanings in the New Testament*. Grand Rapids MI: Baker Book House, 1988.

Efird, James M. *Left Behind? What the Bible Really Says about the End Times*. Macon GA: Smyth & Helwys, 2006.

Fairburn, Patrick. *Commentary on Pastoral Epistles*. Grand Rapids MI: Zondervan, 1956.

Frame, D. M. Translator of *Works by Rabelias*. Berkeley: U. of California Press, 1991.

Gorday, Peter. *Colossians, 1–2 Thessalonians, 1–2 Timothy, Titus, Philemon*. Downers Grove IL: Inter-Varsity Press, 2000.

Harvey, H. H. *Commentary on the Pastoral Epistles—1&2 Timothy*. Philadelphia: American Baptist Publishing House, 1890.

Hovey, Alvah. *An American Commentary on the NT*. Philadelphia: American Baptist Publishing House, 1890.

Kelly, J. N. D. *The Pastoral Epistles*. Hendrickson Publishers, 1993.

Knight, George W. *Commentary on the Pastoral Epistles (New International Greek New Testament)*. Grand Rapids: Eerdmans, 1992.

Leech, Kenneth. *True Prayer.* Harrisberg PA: Morehouse Publishing, 1995.

Liefield, Walter L. *The NIV Application Commentary—1 & 2 Timothy & Titus.* Grand Rapids MI: Zondervan, 1999.

Meeks, Wayne A. *The First Urban Christian.* New Haven & London: Yale University Press, 1983.

Oden, Thomas C. *First & Second Timothy & Titus.* Louisville KY: John Knox Press, 1989.

Rauchenbushe, Walter. *Christianity & the Social Crisis.* Louisville KY: Westminster/John Knox Press, 1991.

Stott, John R. W. *The Message of 1 Timothy & Titus.* Leicester England/Downers Grove IL: Inter-Varsity Press, 1996.

Tench, R. C. *Synonyms of the New Testament.* New York: MacMillan, 1876.

Vennard, Jane E. *A Praying Congregation.* Herndon VA: Alban Institute, 2005.

Wesley, John. *Explanatory Notes Upon the New Testament.* London: Epworth Press, 1954.

Wright, Thomas. *Paul for Everyone—The Pastoral Letters—1 & 2 Timothy & Titus.* London England: The Society for Promoting Christian Knowledge; Louisville KY: John Knox Press, 2004.

Sessions *with*
• • • Peter

Discovering God's *Encouragement*
for the *Christian Journey*

Sarah Jackson Shelton

Sessions *with*
• • • Luke

Following Jesus on the
Journey to Christian Character

Timothy W. Brock

Sessions *with*
Corinthians
• • • Lessons *for the* Imperfect

Michael D. McCullar

Sessions *with*
James •

Explorations *in* Faith *and* Works

Michael D. McCullar

Sessions *with*
• • • Galatians

Finding Freedom *through* Christ

Eric S. Porterfield

Study
the Bible
...a book at a time

The *Sessions Series* is our expanding set of
Bible studies designed to encourage a
deeper encounter with Scripture. Each
volume includes ten lessons as well as
resource pages to facilitate preparation, class
discussion, or individual Bible study.

Now that you have finished your *Sessions
with Timothy and Titus* study, we think you
might be interested in other books from this
series.

**The following pages contain
an excerpt from *Sessions with Luke* by
Timothy W. Brock.**

Coming next:
• *Sessions with Colossians & Philemon — Eric Porterfield*
• *Sessions with Thessalonians — Rickey Letson*

S E S S I O N S *Series*

Call **1-800-747-3016** to order or
visit **www.helwys.com/sessions.**

Character Formed in a Faithful Family

Focal Passages: Luke 1:5-25, 1:26-38,
1:46-56, and 2:41-52

Central Truth of the Session

Personal character is first formed in the context of family. As an infant and as a child, Jesus of Nazareth was raised in a family of dedicated and spiritually-sensitive women and men. In the face of the unusual circumstances that surrounded his birth, these relatives demonstrated faith in God and in God's purposes. By their actions, these people embodied faithfulness and passed that trait on to Jesus.

Parenting as an Act of Faith

In the best of circumstances, birthing and rearing children is an act of faith: faith in parents and family members, faith in the future, and, ultimately, faith in God. As a mother and father gaze at the face of their child sleeping in the cradle, they become aware that this newborn offers the opportunity to redeem the past and to impart cherished hopes and dreams to the next generation. With patience and maturity, the nurture, care, comfort, and protection of a child can become a spiritual discipline that can build and form the character of both parent and child. During the childhood years, it is the responsibility of parents and family members to hand children a heritage. Then, as they mature and gain experience, children can provide parents with new awareness, perception, and insight. In time, if they are open to their children's questions, parents may be challenged anew about life and its varied meanings. The questions of the older child confront parents with their own unanswered and unarticulated issues and dreams (Nelson, 492-93).

In light of the highly unusual circumstances surrounding his conception, the birthing and rearing of Jesus of Nazareth was indeed a profound act of faith. A young woman and various members of her family were asked to demonstrate a remarkable level of faith in themselves, in the future of all humanity, and, ultimately, in God when she became pregnant prior to her marriage. In faith, as this mother gazed at her child in the manger, her personal hopes and dreams for her son were tempered by her knowledge that this child would indeed redeem the past and communicate God's vision for the future. This child's character would develop in a faithful home. From his parents and other members of his family, this child would learn about his rich family and religious heritage. Eventually, this child would grow and mature to the point where he would ask deep questions, questions that caused religious leaders, and even his mother, to reflect on life and faith in fresh ways.

Setting the Context

The focal passages for this lesson were selected from the infancy narratives, Luke 1:5–2:52. As indicated in the introduction to the study, the stories contained in this section of Scripture are found only in the Gospel of Luke. These verses provide the reader of the Gospel with a unique perspective regarding a number of events surrounding the birth of Jesus, a selected event from his childhood, and his family's reactions to all of these events.

Biblical scholars have developed a number of insights regarding the interpretation of these passages. First, scholars have noted the highly personal nature of the stories included in this section of the book. In these passages, intimate images and reflections of members of the holy family are shared in detail. Because of the highly personal content of these stories, some scholars have speculated that Mary or other members of the holy family may have recorded their own stories in a collection of private documents. According to this theory, Luke alone had access to these family diaries as he wrote his Gospel (Culpepper, 7). Second, some scholars speculate that Luke felt compelled to include these unique stories in order to address lingering questions about the circumstances surrounding Jesus' birth, especially with regard to the virgin conception. Third, other scholars believe that the infancy narratives were not included in the earliest versions of the Gospel. These experts speculate that someone other than Luke, again to address specific challenges to Jesus' parentage, added this section later. If these scholars are correct, the Gospel, as Luke wrote it, actually began with Luke 3:1, with both John and Jesus as adults (Craddock, 21).

Regardless of the source of the material or the timing of their writing, these passages provide the reader with unique insights into the family in which Jesus grew up, was nurtured, and first experienced faith.

A Faithful Extended Family

The infancy narratives begin with a remarkable story about members of Jesus' extended family. In Luke 1:5-25, the reader of the Gospel is introduced to Zechariah, a priest of the order of Abijah, and Elizabeth, his wife. Elizabeth, who was also descended from the priestly line of Aaron, was described as a relative, though not necessarily a cousin, of Mary (see Lk 1:36). The couple lived in a Judean town in the hill country (see Lk 1:39). The Scriptures describe Zechariah and Elizabeth as a pious couple, righteous before God and living blamelessly according to the Law. Their piety, however, was juxtaposed against their childlessness. Like Abraham and Sarah before them, the couple was advanced in age and had no child. In that context, it was assumed that the wife was responsible for the failure to have children; the Scriptures concurred with that assessment. Further, barrenness was regarded, at best, a social stigma and, at worst, a sign of God's punishment. The Scriptures implied that the couple lived in the tension between personal piety and public disgrace (Culpepper, 45) (See Lk 1:25).

As a descendant of the priestly class, Zechariah was a member of one of twenty-four divisions of priests. Twice annually, and for a period of one week each time, the members of each division were required to travel to Jerusalem to serve in the Temple. The priests performed a variety of tasks associated with public worship. Their most important task was performing sacrifices on two main altars in the Temple complex. One of these altars was located in a courtyard outside the sanctuary. In this public venue, the people could watch the priest as he led in worship. A second altar was located inside the sanctuary, out of public view. Twice each day, while the people prayed, sacrifices were offered and incense was burned simultaneously on these two altars. The priests would typically draw lots to determine which of the two altars each would serve. It was considered a high honor to be selected to serve the inner altar (45-46).

On one occasion, Zechariah was chosen to perform the sacrifices and burn the incense on the altar in the inner sanctuary. In that high and holy place, while performing a sacred function, Zechariah encountered the angel Gabriel, a messenger sent from the presence of God. Not surprisingly, Zechariah was overwhelmed and fearful. Gabriel offered words of comfort, words of promise, and words of mild rebuke to the frightened priest. The words of comfort were "Do not be afraid for your prayers have been answered" (see Lk 1:11). The words of promise came in four parts:

- You and your wife will have a son whom you will name John.
- The birth of this child will bring great joy and gladness to you, your wife, and to many others because he will be favored by God.
- You will raise your son according to the Nazirite vows (see Numbers 6:3 and Judges 13:2-5).
- Your son will speak with a prophetic voice like Elijah and will prepare the people for the coming of the Lord (Craddock, 26).

The mild rebuke came when Zechariah questioned the words of promise. Even a pious and faithful man such as Zechariah found it hard to believe that he and Elizabeth could have a child. When he questioned the prophecy, Gabriel informed him that he would be unable to speak until the day the prophecy was fulfilled, i.e., the birth of the child.

Outside, in the courtyard of the Temple, the people were waiting for Zechariah to emerge from the inner sanctum and to pronounce a blessing. When he finally came out, he was unable to speak. Crude sign language was inadequate to communicate what had happened. The people concluded, correctly, that he must have experienced some form of vision while in the inner sanctuary. Awed by his encounter and still unable to speak, the dutiful priest completed his tour of duty and returned home.

In spite of his initial skepticism, Zechariah and Elizabeth conceived a child. It was then time for Elizabeth to be overwhelmed by the good news of the impending birth. She secluded herself from the community, from the same people who had viewed her with disgrace. Instead of proclaiming the news from the rooftops, she chose to privately reflect on her great fortunes. Zechariah was mute but obedient. Elizabeth was pregnant and cloistered. Both members of Jesus' extended family were faithful in unbelievable circumstances. Their faith culminated in the birth of their son, John (see Lk 1:57-80).

A Risky Faithfulness

In the Annunciation of the Birth of Jesus, Luke 1:26-38, the Gospel writer recorded a second story of faith in the context of unbelievable circumstances. In some ways, the situation described in this second narrative is similar to the situation outlined in the first story:

Zechariah and Elizabeth were both described as pious and righteous people. The same description applied to Mary. In various verses in the infancy narratives, Mary is described as "thoughtful" (1:29), "favored by God" and obedient (1:30), believing and worshipful (1:46-55), and devoted to Jewish law and piety (2:22-51).

In his encounter with Gabriel, Zechariah received a four-part promise. In her encounter with Gabriel, Mary received a series of promises. First, the angel told her that she would have a son and that his name would be Jesus. Second, he promised that the child would be called "the Son of the Most High" and that he would reign on the throne of his ancestor (by adoption), David. Third, the angel assured Mary that she would conceive through the power of the Holy Spirit and that, because of this unique conception, the child would be holy. And fourth, the angel offered Elizabeth's pregnancy as a sign of God's ability to follow through with these promises.

In some ways, the situation described in this second story is different from the dynamics in the first story:

In the first story, the stigma of barrenness was removed as a pious, married couple was finally able to conceive. The resulting birth led to celebration in the community and speculation about the mission of the child, John. In the second story, the stigma of pregnancy outside of marriage hung over the head of an engaged teenager. The resulting birth occurred in obscurity, but with heavenly celebrations.

In the first story, a righteous priest encountered an angel in a holy place—the inner sanctuary of the Temple in Jerusalem—while performing a religious ritual, with many witnesses waiting outside. Zechariah would have been a logical recipient of an angelic visitation. In the second story, a righteous peasant girl encountered an angel in an ordinary place—the backwater town of Nazareth— under ordinary circumstances, with no witnesses. Mary was a most unlikely candidate to be used by God for such an important task.

In the first story, the righteous priest questioned the good news spoken by the angel, received a mild rebuke, and experienced the loss of voice. In the second story, the peasant girl accepted the challenge without reservation, in spite of the possible consequences of being pregnant before marriage. (Refer to Deut 22:13-29 for a detailed explanation of the consequences of sexual activity outside the context of marriage.)

Seeking Support from Extended Family

While Zechariah lost his voice as a result of his momentary lack of faith, Mary found a unique voice when she readily accepted God's calling for her life. She used this voice to sing a song of praise which is recorded in Luke 1:46-55.

Mary's song is recorded in the context of a broader passage of Scripture titled the Visitation, Luke 1:39-56. In this passage, the Gospel writer reported that, after the announcement of the birth of Jesus, Mary left Nazareth to visit Elizabeth in the Judean hill country (see Lk 39-41a). Some biblical scholars speculate that Mary initiated this visit in order to ascertain the validity of the angel's prophecy about Elizabeth. According to this approach, the only way to see if Elizabeth was indeed pregnant was for Mary to make a visit to her relative. Commentator Fred Craddock discounts this theory. He believes that Mary had already accepted Gabriel's word as gospel truth. Craddock believes Mary was drawn to Elizabeth by a common experience and for mutual support. It was simply a case of one family member needing the company of another (29).

When Mary arrived at the home of Zechariah and Elizabeth, she offered words of greeting to her hostess. Verses 41b-45 record an "inspired speech" delivered by Elizabeth upon hearing this greeting. A spiritually-sensitive person, Elizabeth was overwhelmed by Mary's presence. Filled with the Holy Spirit, Elizabeth praised both Mary and her unborn child. She blessed Mary on two grounds. First, Elizabeth exalted Mary because she had been chosen to be the mother of the Lord. Second, Elizabeth affirmed Mary because she had immediately believed the promise of God and had responded in humility to the responsibility.

Mary's response to this outpouring of the Spirit was to give voice to her own feelings in song. Traditionally, this song, recorded in Luke 1:46-55, has been identified as the Magnificat, so termed from the opening word in the Latin translation. (Note: Some scholars have speculated that this passage was heavily influenced by the prayer of Hannah found in 1 Samuel 2:1-10 [Tolbert, 24]). The first section of the passage is autobiographical. In verses 46-49, Mary offers personal words of praise to God for the special favor

God bestowed on her, even though she is a handmaiden of low estate. The remainder of the passage expands these words of personal testimony to demonstrate a general principle about the nature of God and the pattern of God's relationship with humanity. Verses 50-55 develop the idea that God's selection of Mary anticipated and modeled what God would do for the poor, the powerless, and the oppressed of the world. In these verses, Mary extols the God who will bring down the mighty and exalt those of low degree, the God who will fill the hungry and send the rich away empty. In the final analysis, the unexpected choice of Mary to fulfill this unique role in God's plan mirrored the complete reversal of fortunes that would characterize the ultimate fulfillment of God's promises to Israel and to all humanity.

In Luke 1:56, the visitation story ends with a simple statement. Mary stayed with Elizabeth for three months, presumably through the birth of John, and then returned to her own home (Craddock, 29-31).

Faithfulness Embodied in the Child of a Dedicated Family

The story of Jesus in the temple, Luke 2:41-52, is the only Gospel account of a childhood experience in the life of Jesus.

Why tell did Luke choose to include this story in his Gospel? Biblical scholars speculate that, in both the dedication of Jesus in the Temple (Lk 2:21-38) and in this passage, Luke attempted to establish two facts: first, that Jesus' family actively and faithfully practiced the Jewish faith, and second, that, from birth, Jesus was thoroughly grounded in the heritage and rituals of Judaism. In sharing the dedication stories, Luke demonstrated that Joseph and Mary followed the rituals associated with the birth of a first-born, male child (see Lev 12:2-8). In relating the story of Jesus in the Temple, Luke reported the fact that the family made annual pilgrimages to Jerusalem for religious festivals. As outlined in Exodus 23:14-17, all male Israelites, and by implications their families, should travel each year to Jerusalem to celebrate the festivals of Passover, Pentecost, and Tabernacles. If the family lived at some distance from Jerusalem, all efforts should be made to celebrate at least Passover in Jerusalem. In the end, the passages convey the impression that, as good, Jewish parents, Joseph and Mary both practiced the faith and modeled the faith for their son.

This passage describes the annual pilgrimage to Jerusalem for the Passover Festival during the year that Jesus was twelve years old. At age twelve, it was unlikely that Jesus had yet participated in the Jewish rituals signaling the transition from childhood to adulthood. But as an older child, Jesus would have been given some measure of independence both during their journey to and from Jerusalem and during their stay in the city. While in Jerusalem, Jesus may have been allowed to explore the city with friends and relatives, checking in with his parents on occasion. At the conclusion of the festival, Joseph and Mary began their trip back home, assuming that Jesus was somewhere in the group of travelers. Moving at a pace of fifteen miles a day, their journey from Jerusalem to Nazareth should have taken four or five days (Culpepper, 76). Their journey was cut short when they discovered that Jesus was not in the caravan.

The anxious parents retraced their steps up the steep hill that led to the city. For three fear-filled days, they searched in vain for their wayward child. At last, they discovered their son on the grounds of the Temple complex. In all probability, Jesus had joined a small group of rabbis in one of the side halls adjacent to the outer courts of the complex. Using a Socratic approach to teaching, that is, asking questions, soliciting individual answers, and critiquing the responses, these rabbis and their students would spend hours in spirited debate. As a novice, Jesus would not have played a prominent role of leadership in these discussions, but the Scriptures indicate that the rabbis were amazed with his understanding and his responses. For a child raised by a peasant family and educated in a provincial synagogue, Jesus was astonishing (Gilmour, 67).

His behavior also astonished his anxious parents, particularly his mother. The same Mary who had once so readily accepted the words of promise offered by Gabriel so many years before was now a fretting parent who had not seen her son for at least four days! The same Mary who had once sung the praises of God for her role in God's redemption of humanity was now the mother of an inconsiderate child! In a rather terse rebuke, Mary chided Jesus: "Child, why have you treated us like this? Look, your father and I have been searching for you in great anxiety" (Lk 2:48b, NRSV).

The Scriptures imply that Jesus was also astonished at his mother's response to the situation. In paraphrase, he said, "You, above all others, should have known where I would be. I now understand what you have known all along; I must be in my Father's house, doing my Father's business." According to Craddock, this passage demonstrates that, at age twelve, Jesus had already claimed for himself a unique relationship to God. To this point, other people had proclaimed and celebrated this relationship: in the angel Gabriel's annunciation to Mary, in Elizabeth's reaction to Mary's visit, and in Simeon's and Anna's reaction to Jesus during his dedication in the Temple (see Lk 2:22-38). Now, in the context of parental anxiety and disappointment, Jesus demonstrated faithfulness to God and to God's purposes as he claimed his own unique relationship to God and his special responsibilities (Craddock, 42).

The Scriptures stated that Joseph and Mary did not understand their son's response or reaction to their concerns. Nonetheless, Jesus returned home with his family while Mary "treasured all these things in her heart" (Lk 2:51, NRSV). As Jesus continued to grow and mature in the context of his dedicated peasant family, he demonstrated the faithfulness that he had seen embodied in his parents and members of his family. God and others smiled on the person that he was becoming. In his response to his parents in the Temple and in the process of becoming the man God had called him to be, Jesus demonstrated an important truth: family love and loyalties have their place and flourish when the higher love and loyalty go to God.

Summary of the Session

The environment created in the home, the values espoused there, and the behaviors exhibited in everyday living set the stage for the faith development of children. The focal passages selected for this lesson explored how family faithfulness, even in the face of unbelievable circumstances and risky consequences, helped to shape the character of Jesus as a child.

1. Based on your reading of the lesson's focal passages and background material, write a definition of the term "faithfulness."

_____
_____
_____
_____
_____
_____

2. How did Zechariah and Elizabeth each embody and model faithfulness to God's calling?

_____
_____
_____
_____
_____
_____

3. How did Mary embody and model faithfulness to God's calling?

_____
_____
_____
_____
_____
_____

4. Reflecting on your own experience, identify one or two members of your extended family or your church family who have embodied and modeled faithfulness to God's calling for you. Describe that person or persons. Then describe in as much detail as possible how their faithfulness has impacted your life and character.

_____
_____
_____
_____
_____